Quality management in education

Quality management in education

Sustaining the vision
through
action research

Edited by
Pamela Lomax

London and New York

Hyde
Publications

First published 1996
by Routledge
11 New Fetter Lane, London EC4P 4EE

and Hyde Publications
57 Exeter Road, Bournemouth BH2 5AF

Simultaneously published in the USA and Canada
by Routledge
29 West 35th Street, New York, NY 10001

Routledge is an International Thomson Publishing company

© 1996 Pamela Lomax and on behalf of the individual authors

Typeset in Palatino by Alan Hyde, Hyde Publications
Printed and bound in Great Britain by
TJ Press (Padstow) Ltd, Padstow, Cornwall

British Library Cataloguing in Publication Data
A catalogue record for this book is available from the
British Library

Library of Congress Cataloguing in Publication Data
A catalogue record for this book has been requested.

ISBN 0–415–15252–6 (hbk)
ISBN 0–415–15253–4 (pbk)

Contents

List of illustrations

Contributors to the book

Doug Bone, Headteacher,
Wandle Valley School,
Welbeck Road,
SM3 1LP

Moyra Evans, Deputy Head Teacher,
Denbigh School,
Burchard Avenue,
Milton Keynes,
Bucks
MK3 7HU

Di Hannon, Senior Lecturer in Science Education,
School of Education,
Kingston University,
Kingston Hill,
Kingston upon Thames,
KT2 7LB

John Loftus, Head Teacher,
Mayfield Primary School,
Mayfield Road,
Hanwell,
London
W7 3RT

Pamela Lomax, Professor of Educational Research,
School of Education,
Kingston University,
Kingston Hill,
Kingston upon Thames,
LT2 7LB

Dawn McKen,
Guildford College of Further and Higher Education,
Stoke Park,
Guildford,
GU1 1EZ

Marian Nicholas,
Learning Support Teacher,
30 St James Avenue,
Hampton Hill
TW1 1HH

Zoe Parker, Lecturer in Education,
School of Education,
Kingston University,
Kingston Hill,
Kingston upon Thames,
KT2 7LB

Jon Stevens, Head Teacher,
Eastwick Middle School,
Eastwick Drive,
Bookham,
Surrey
KT23 3PP

Jack Whitehead, Lecturer in Education,
School of Education,
University of Bath,
Claverton Down,
Bath,
Avon
BA2 7AY

Cathie Woodward, School of Education,
School of Education,
Anglia Polytechnic University,
Victoria Road South,
Chelmsford,
Essex
CM1 1LL

Introduction

Jean McNiff

Action research is about active learning, not only the learning of substantial concepts, but also learning how to learn - getting to grips with the process of deliberately changing how one thinks. In this sense, learning can be problematic. Many of us, I believe, resist the invitation to learn. I am quite sure about my own reaction to many invitations to active learning: I resist them. Active learning is disquieting and destabilising; it implies a revisiting and reappraisal of where we are, a challenge to the validity and use value of our current thinking, and a conscious decision to let it go if necessary. The new mental matter that replaces the old becomes the new status quo, until that also is subjected to a critical scrutiny of its validity and use value in our lives ... and so it continues. The process of transformation becomes the norm; change acquires its own stability. It is not surprising that we often refuse to learn. It is much more comfortable to stay as we are, even though we might recognise this as the sluggish slide to inertia. While many of us might embrace the rhetoric of the need for continuing learning, we might not always live it out in practice. Whether or not we actively learn is our choice. The trick is to be aware of the choice, and to choose with responsibility. Having chosen, we then must act on our decision.

This book is about people who are vitally aware of their own need to learn, and to apply that learning to the process of facilitating other people's learning. It is a book about change, not in the sense that change is an isolated singularity, or a string of isolated singularities, that might suddenly enter the stream of consciousness; but of change being the nature of that stream of consciousness. As we live we are in a continuing process of transformation, engaging in a form of thinking that is transformatory, and that transforms our social practices.

For such change to carry the imperative of quality, as the legend on the back of this book suggests, the change must be for the better; it must be improvement. Improvement is linked inextricably with the notion of education, with the idea of openness to new possibilities, of responsible choice in diversity. Such is the nature of the stories in this book. Each story describes how its author deliberately changed an aspect of practice in the service of the people in their care. Such deliberateness implies a willingness to change; such 'morally committed action', in the words of Pam Lomax, itself is aimed at improvement. The improvement is hard won. It is won at the expense of personal turmoil, of questioning comfortable ways of thinking, of personal instability in the transformatory practice of critical self-appraisal. That process, implicit in these stories, is a precursor to a better, more humane world.

The book is also a story about people's stories. It is the story of how people may be supported in their professional learning by others who care enough to engage in the kind of support practice that requires them also to learn. This is the nature of the professional network that is facilitated by Pam Lomax at Kingston University. Pam is internationally recognised as one of the foremost proponents of professional education through action research, and her stature as a supporter of innovative forms of collaborative enquiry is substantial. Such recognition is also not without cost. In her commitment to promoting the cause of the legitimacy of practitioners' knowledge, to challenging traditional theorising and elitist forms of knowledge, Pam Lomax has accepted the mandate constantly to interrogate her own ideas, to stand accountable for her own practice. That story is here, too.

The multiple-embedded stories of the book are echoes of the multiple-embedded lives of the storytellers within their network. The motif is clear - people deeply committed to improving the quality of their own practice in the service of others; and showing how they do it; and standing accountable for their actions. We should all learn from these stories, those of us who are willing to learn, and who recognise the need also to strive to improve our own practice.

Content of the book

The first chapter by Pam Lomax, Jack Whitehead and Moyra Evans, is very important, not only in setting the scene for this book, but also in challenging deeply-rooted assumptions in the wider community of educational researchers about the nature of what constitutes an educational epistemology. The authors are committed to practitioner research as an effective way of improving the quality of education and its management. They discuss different ideas about quality and reach the conclusion that validated accounts of practitioner research not only demonstrate ways of achieving excellence in the practice and management of education, but can contribute to a new epistemology of practice.

In chapter 2, Doug Bone, Headteacher of a Special School for children with emotional and behavioural needs, considers how he might improve his practice by aiming for collegiate management. In 1992 a school inspection challenged his belief that the school was managed collegially and queried whether this was an effective style of management. Doug had to manage the contradiction of needing to influence others, while wanting them to contribute independently to a democratic organisation. The chapter describes how action research forced him to question his own management practice and led him to develop strategies to increase the involvement of his senior staff in managing the school and building their confidence so that they could involve others.

Dawn McKen describes in chapter 3 a collaborative exercise to encourage ownership by staff of the monitoring and evaluation process in a College of Further Education. The impetus for this research was provided by the introduction of a college-wide monitoring and evaluation system into the College. This coincided with the appointment of a new Principal, and a consequent restructuring of the college organisation in which Dawn became the manager of a newly formed Quality Development Unit. She viewed quality as a key success criterion, and sought to foster a culture of quality within the college where the skills of all employees could be harnessed, and a collaborative ethos could become the norm. The chapter details how she applied an action research methodology within the context of the monitoring and evaluation process to work towards her goal.

A focus on pupil behaviour to introduce Total Quality Management in a middle school is offered by Jon Stevens in chapter 4. The study began with Jon's attempt to apply some of the principles of TQM to raise standards in the middle school of which he was a head. His initial focus was to be the work of the senior management team, but this soon led to his being challenged both by his action research support group and by his own senior management team to find a focus that was less at odds with the principles of TQM he sought to introduce. Instead of his initial plan, he used the idea of an inverted pyramid to identify the logical focus of action as a whole school project about improving pupil behaviour.

How can one enhance the image of a school to meet the demands of an ever competitive situation in such a way as to remain true to educational values? In chapter 5, John Loftus describes how, as an acting headteacher of a multi-ethnic first school in an outer London Borough threatened with falling rolls, he was faced with the dilemma of having to market his school while believing that marketing was unprofessional and unethical. He disliked the idea that schools were in competition with each other, were selling their curriculum. As his project developed he came to see that. marketing could be interpreted differently; that communicating with parents and enhancing school community relations all involved marketing an image of the school. The chapter describes some of the strategies that John developed to reverse the threat of falling rolls.

Marian Nicholas worked as a support teacher in a middle school in an Outer London Borough to carry out her action research into understanding the changing gender dynamics in a mixed ability classroom. In chapter 6 she tells how she worked for two terms with a class of ten year old boys and girls and their teacher, Jo, to implement a non-sexist classroom within mixed ability teaching to enhance equal opportunity for all pupils. The research came about because she had become conscious of the fact that she had become an example of the concept of a living contradiction, negating her educational values in her practice, because she failed to offer a curriculum that met the needs of a mixed ability class and had found a 'hidden' sexist curriculum in her classroom. The chapter tells of her efforts to overcome the contradiction.

Chapter 7 is about preparing student teachers to respond to special educational needs. During 1994, Di Hannon worked with first year teacher training students to prepare science boxes for children who were being taught at home or in hospital. A 'science box' is a portable self-contained resource box containing science activities and materials matched to part of the science national curriculum and sufficiently flexible to use in a variety of teaching situations. The intention behind the action research was to promote student teachers' understanding of the needs of pupils with a range of physical and sensory special needs whilst training them within the constraints of the college primary science syllabus.

Chapter 8 is about using story to develop explanations about staff development in a secondary school department. Moyra Evans, in her role as deputy headteacher responsible for staff development, worked with Department A for a year to help them review what was happening in their classrooms so as to improve children's learning. This chapter focuses on her exploration of the use of story in in-service sessions to facilitate discussion of sensitive issues. By presenting her own story, Moyra hoped that it would act as a catalyst for her colleagues to write their stories and in doing so explore their own practice and make discoveries about it.

Pam Lomax and Moyra Evans describe in chapter 9 what working in partnership to implement teacher education can look like, when the research is undertaken honestly from a partnership point of view, instead of within the traditional power relationships of teacher education. They show how they actively supported each other in developing their ideas, both of their own practice and of the other's. In this very unusual piece, they explain the processes they underwent in order to demonstrate the way that they improved their work, both through self-reflection and through inter subjective reflection, where each acted as a mirror to the other to reflect back the externalised self-reflections that were emerging. The partnership between school and university which forms the focus of this work won recognition through the RSA Partnership Awards in 1994.

Chapter 10 offers a Higher Education perspective on critical friends, collaborative working and strategies for effecting quality. The paper is written by Pam Lomax, Cathie Woodward and Zoe Parker from the perspective of tutors in HE whose job it is to facilitate managers' action research. The managers who work in various areas of Education are engaged in action research towards a masters degree. As part of this, they are expected to establish a working relationship with a colleague who will provide supportive but critical friendship during the period of the research, and who will take part in a meeting set up in the University to validate the research. The chapter reports on original research about the role of the critical friend and the skills of collaborative working in the context of implementing quality through action research.

Evaluating the book: 'walking the talk'

Excerpts from the book in draft were used as part of inservice courses organised by Pam Lomax at Kingston University in January, 1996. Chapter 1 in particular was taken as a starting point for teachers to develop their own conceptualisation of an epistemology of practice. There was some interesting reaction. First, the meeting was mistrustful of the title. There seems to be an assumption in educational circles that issues of quality are bound up with the concept of Total Quality Management. This is not so. Yet this reaction is significant and emphasises the need for the development of texts like this. Concepts such as TQM suggest that quality is something ensured by managers operating within traditional hierarchical systems; that it is the implementation of policy, and the monitoring of the outcomes of implementation strategies. Yet quality in education, and in the management of education does not happen by leaving the process to managers and so-called experts. Meaningful change is brought about by individuals taking action to change their own situations, and making their practice more relevant to those they are serving.

Another comment was that the book was not sufficiently critical. This is interesting, because the idea of critique in action research is seen through the practices of individuals who review their work with the intention of changing it. Action research carries an immanent critique, in the sense that people are challenged not only to question the practices of others, but actively to question their own assumptions, the very ground on which they stand. This means stepping back and reflecting on practice, and also reflecting on the thought structures that inform that practice. The idea of active learning in the first paragraph is important here. Learning is the deliberate challenge of taken-for-granted assumptions. It is recognising that whatever we do is already framed by previous learning and conditioning. Action research enables us to be aware of that; while we cannot ever be free of the legacy of our own history and culture, at least we can be aware of our own situatedness within that history and culture, and accept that there are differences that need to be celebrated, other possible futures that we are invited to consider. The stories in the book demonstrate that struggle on the part of the authors, how they challenged their own situatedness, and resolved to change aspects of practice where they could.

The critique is not in the editor's commentary on the stories of others; it is within those stories, the narratives of people working through their own critique, and showing what critique looks like in its lived reality.

Now, over to you

This is an important book. Its purpose is to share the work of a number of educators in schools and colleges who have used action research to improve the quality of their organisations and classrooms. Common to all the accounts is the idea that values underpin educational work; that an inner vision has to be articulated and shared by others, whether colleagues or students.

The approaches described in the book are becoming increasingly influential, and offer a new kind of in-service practice that enables practitioners to be in charge of their own lives. The book is also highly practical, and can inspire educators at the chalk face to experiment with new ideas.

This is the invitation to you. As you read and reflect, think how these ideas might impact on your own life. Try them out; revise and adapt. Become part of the network of people thinking, sharing good practice, and sharing again. Write your own story, and put that out for public access. It is through our contribution to the development of such a culture of conscious sharing, transparency and learning that we qualify as critically self-reflective practitioners who are committed to responsible action in the service of others.

Chapter 1

Contributing to an epistomology of quality management practice

Pamela Lomax, Jack Whitehead and Moyra Evans

> Knowing ignorance is strength.
> Ignoring knowledge is sickness.
> If one is sick of sickness, then one is not sick.
> *Lao Tsu*

For many in Education, quality has become a term that is identified with bureaucratic procedures or institutional practices for monitoring the effectiveness of organisational systems. There are many books that describe these quality management systems and define different quality control mechanisms such as quality assurance, quality audit and quality assessment (Doherty, 1994; Parsons, 1994). Other books emphasise the importance of measuring quality and concern themselves with indicators of quality (Riley and Nuttall, 1994). Some of these books put forward ideas that have their origin in industrial settings. For example a popular view of quality which has an industrial origin is the idea of total quality management (Collard, 1989) which has been applied to schools (Murgatroyd and Morgan, 1993; Greenwood and Gaunt, 1994) and higher education institutions (Lewis and Smith, 1994). Murgatroyd and Morgan described a quality revolution in which the right to define quality has moved from the experts to the customers. They suggest that we should view schools and colleges as inverted pyramids in which parents and pupils, as the customers, should be put at the top, teachers at the chalk face would go next, and the senior managers would come at the bottom, with the headteacher in the position of the inverted apex. This sounds great until one reads between the lines of statements such as 'this book is not intended to discuss the ideology of schooling, but to sensitise and help those now leading primary and secondary schools to understand and respond to new contexts that governments have legislated' (Murgatroyd and Morgan, 1993:2). In other words, such a view of quality excludes what we have come to understand as praxis or morally committed action (Wildman, 1995), which would emphasise a critical approach to practices seen to deny social justice rather than a blind acceptance of legislation and a technical response to it. This is not to say that educational managers should not do their best within contexts over which they have little control, but to deplore the idea that quality management can only focus on the means and make little comment about the ends!

We find it difficult in our work in schools and higher education to identify with the language of the market place, which is used in many of these examples. Like Tasker and Packham (1993), in their excellent analysis of markets and higher education, we do not see our students as customers in the sense that they know what they want and can buy it from us. More importantly, these mechanisms for determining quality do not make explicit the educational imperatives that are necessary if applied in educational institutions. They exclude what we would see as the most important vehicle for quality, what could be called self-driven quality, which is the process through which we attempt to live our educational values in our practice as educational managers.

It might be helpful to clarify our position in relation to the six ideas that West-Burnham and Davies (1994:4-5) used to shape their frame of reference about quality approaches that schools have taken from industry.

❏   Their first idea was that quality is defined by customer needs. If this means that we should hold ourselves responsible for the values we attempt to embody in our professional practice, and that we share a value about helping our students to find meaning and purpose in their educational lives, we agree.

❏   Their second idea was that quality is defined in terms of fitness for purpose. We produce accounts of our practice in public fora for validation and identify this process as an action research approach. If this is fitness for purpose, we must emphasise that it is our purpose, as professional educators, not a market-defined purpose.

❏   We would agree with their third idea that quality is achieved through continuous improvement, as long as this is conceived as a process, but find there is a tension between this and their fourth and fifth ideas.

❏   Their fourth idea is that quality is managed through prevention not direction and their fifth idea is that quality is about 'getting it right first time'. We agree that individuals are autonomous professionals, and as such are capable of making the practical judgements that would help support these ideas; but prevention conjures up a deficit model, whereas we would want to support a continuous professional development model based on living values. 'Getting it right first time' under-emphasises the complexity of those judgments that are necessary for educational work, including educational management work.

❏   We think that finding quality in educational provision is not about measuring outcomes, which is their sixth and final idea. It is more about the formative evaluation of practice that both leads to and contains within itself a practical knowledge of what quality means (Lomax,1989b). This is not because we undervalue outcomes or the importance of knowing what has been achieved, but because we believe that the nature of educational work demands a continuous shifting of the goalposts to incorporate a living educational outcome and that action research offers us an appropriate way of researching our attempts to improve the quality of such living educative processes.

Many commentaries on quality management in education, like that of West-Burnham and Davies have included quality control aspects alongside value based aspects (Mann and Pedler,1992; Aspin, Chapman and Wilkinson, 1994). For example, in writing about quality practice, Alexander (1992) listed five considerations that we would support. These were that we might consider the values and beliefs we hold about what it means to be educated; the empirical evidence about effectiveness in delivering learning; the conceptual picture of teaching, learning and curriculum relations; the political imperatives of client community and state expectations; and the pragmatic consideration of what it is possible to do in a particular context. We think that all these considerations are important in quality educational management and not just the last one as is often assumed.

In the context of this advice we might consider the national context of the management of the continuing professional development of teachers in terms of *the grounds* for improving the quality and professionalism of teachers. The government has accepted the advice of the teacher training agency (TTA,1995) on creating a better focused, strategic, approach to continuing professional development. The aim is to develop agreed national standards to help teachers and schools set targets for teachers' development and career provision and to help focus and improve training programmes at national, local and school level. One focus for this work will be the establishment of agreed standards of excellence in the classroom. In this context we think we need to operationalise a research-based model of quality management which will promote the development and understanding of these standards rather than statistical performance indicators. Because of the nature of education and the changing social context, it is inconceivable that standards can be prescribed in tablets of stone and remain operational. So we argue that we need to develop an epistemology or theory of the grounds of professional knowledge that would be appropriate for generating standards that are flexible and situated rather than absolute.

Good quality educational research

We propose that quality educational management is more likely to emerge from quality educational research than from quality control systems. We recognise that there are different points of view about what counts as good quality research and that not all research about education is educational research. We define educational research in terms of educational standards and criteria. Non-educational research would include research undertaken within the frameworks and procedures of the social sciences which apply sociological, psychological, historical and other criteria. We are not questioning the legitimacy of this research within its own frames of reference. Indeed we have been impressed by Wexler's recent contribution to a social theory of education (Wexler, 1995). However, we do not think that such a disciplines approach can produce valid descriptions and explanations for the educational development of individuals.

We find that our values do not permit us to accept as 'educational' what some individuals and groups define as educational. For example, we think it would be immoral as well as uneducational to be engaged in research that suggested a way of ending an injustice, and defer putting this solution into effect until the research was completed. Equally unacceptable to us is the position of the armchair philosopher whose deductive theorising lacks grounding in the research context, so that the theory is remote and irrelevant. An over emphasis on methodology can also lead to mediocrity because researchers become dominated by technical concerns that detract from the purpose of the research. Whilst we accept that 'good quality', in both social science research and educational research, can be defined in terms of information gathering and in terms of the creation and testing of theory, we want to resist the idea that educational research can be defined **solely** in these terms. Our resistance stems from our view that educational research, in producing descriptions and explanations for the educational development of individuals, could involve the justification and use of spiritual, aesthetic and ethical judgements as well as the systematic and scientific forms of enquiry that constitute social science.

Unfortunately many inappropriate definitions of educational research are the result of its control by interest groups that have a stake in maintaining exclusive claims to knowledge that are divorced from the purpose and processes of education (Torbert, 1981). In these cases existing power relations are maintained through the enforcement of particular procedures which are used to determine what counts as research and what research is supported, funded and published (Foucault, 1977, 1980; Habermas, 1976; Whitehead, 1993; Lomax, 1994d).

The idea of 'fitness for purpose' could usefully apply to deciding whether a social science or an educational research approach is most appropriate. Our discussion in this paper is about educational management research within the context of the teaching profession in our own culture. We recognise that our brand of educational action research is not exclusive and there are other value-based positions on educational research that we would accept. For example we think that Carr and Kemmis (1986) provided a useful description of educational research in their characterisation of action research that emphasised a self-reflective enquiry undertaken by practitioners to improve the rationality and justice of their educational practices, their understanding of these practices and the situations in which these practices occurred. We agree with most of this but would exclude their emphasis on rationality, which for us is only one of several criteria that are of equal and often greater importance than rationality.

What constitutes good quality educational research within our framework? We judge good quality educational research by the quality of the claims to educational knowledge it produces, the quality of the processes from which these claims emerge and the nature of the criteria which can be used to test the validity of the claims.

For us, educational research is a vocation. It is a value-laden form of enquiry which we use in giving some meaning and purpose to our lives as educators. In this sense the imagined solution, the practical outcomes, the improved practice, the contribution to a better life, lead both methodology and theory. In action research the means (method and theory) and ends (improved practice) merge into each other. Methodology in good quality action research is not a technical activity, but a way of ensuring a valid link between your descriptions and explanations and your practice. Methodology is not simply data collection. It should provide a practical guide to implementing some principles you would wish to apply to your research. For example:

> I, Pam, have written about the importance of participation and collaboration in affirming the democratic and relational values that underpin action research and made suggestions about how you can develop co-researcher relationships, critical friendships and support groups (Lomax, 1991:102-113).
>
> I, Jack, have argued for the importance of testing the validity of the claims that action researchers make about their practice and made suggestions about how you can convene carefully constituted validation groups to help test out your claims (Whitehead, 1993).
>
> I, Moyra, have written about the importance of recognising feeling and the emotions in order to develop a better understanding of my own practice and suggested how you could use fictionalised writing to explore these aspects (Evans, 1995b).

Our point is that forming particular research relationships, participating in validation groups, and writing stories are strategies that are part of the rich methodology of action research but are also intimately linked and incapable of separation from theorising about it or from its aims and practical outcomes. All these elements help constitute our living educational theories. Perhaps it would help to clarify our meanings if we now share with you the way that we characterise educational action research.

Pam's position on educational research

I have previously outlined what I see as the characteristics of educational research as distinct from social science (Lomax, 1994d:12-14) but I would like to explore these characteristics in terms of my own educational values.

Good quality educational research for me should be tentative research. This is because my 'education' is a continuing process in which I can come to know but never achieve the final completed state. This is linked to my idea of 'vulnerability' where I recognise my own lack of knowledge and am willing to admit this to others. I value this kind of humility and recognise a particular difficulty in living it in management practice.

In my view research should be done by educational managers themselves and not necessarily by so-called experts. I like the way that Mary Gurney (1989) argues that the researcher should be both innovator and implementer; the one who poses the questions and the one who investigates the solutions. I value this way of empowering professionals. This also relates to what I see as an ethical-professional dimension. I think educational research has to include in its doing an educational outcome; it has to address the issue of its own motives and explain what is meant by improvement in immediate professional terms. This is one reason why I characterise educational research as insider research. It implies that the manager-researcher will engage in a continuing critique of her own educational management values as part of the research process as she seeks answers to the questions that her management practices pose. I value the moral autonomy of this position.

Being an insider to the research is crucially significant for me because my aim is for the research to be educational in the sense of self-developing. It is through enquiring into my own management practice that I am able to create a living form of educational management theory that is constituted by the descriptions and explanations that I produce as I answer questions such as, 'How do I improve what I am doing?' This is important to me because I value the opportunity to be able to engage in learning.

I think educational management research should be practical. I have little patience with research that does not inform what I am doing. I think that intervention in my own management practice to bring about improvement is extremely practical. This does not mean that my research is concerned merely with technical matters. I view practical research in terms of the practical ethic discussed by Adelman (1989) where educational purposes and means are addressed together making for informed, committed action (praxis). For me, practical does not exclude theoretical, but locates theoretical in a practical context of ongoing professional evaluation and action. I value action and intervention and believe it should always be intentional and committed.

I want my research to be authentic so that other educational managers are able to recognise it for what it is and empathise with my underpinning values. I dislike deception and manipulation of others. I see my emphasis on the importance of co-researching rather than treating others as respondents or informants as related to my wish to empower others in the research relationship. I like to enable others to speak for themselves rather than interpreting their positions for them, although I am happy to facilitate their understanding where I can.

I think research should be rigorous. I think it is more difficult to work with 'subjective' data than with 'objective' data and therefore educational management research, with its emphasis on values and action, demands high level research skills. This has important implications for the idea of validity, which is about being able to make a plausible case for one's research claims before an 'educated' audience of peers. But we can get too obsessed with the notion of validity and there is a danger in attempting to codify the grounds or criteria for validity too closely because we are likely to lose a sense of our own tentativeness. I value commitment, openness and a quest for truth.

Most important for me is that research should be holistic. As a teacher educator, investigating my own practice, I do not separate my intent to motivate my students from my intent to help them develop their technical competence, from my intent to help them refine their professional judgement. I value respect for the whole person, which I think means treating professional knowledge holistically. I object to the way in which particular practices are separated into higher order skills and lower order skills, and to the way in which certain powerful interest groups lay claim to the former, like Fenstermacher's (1992) idea that schools are places where teachers can learn technical competence (the systemics of schooling) but universities are places where they might learn to acquire knowledge of the educative purposes of schooling. His 'elitist' views make me feel ashamed when I read what Erica Holley says of academics:

> Teachers are seduced by academics who simultaneously include and exclude us in their writing about teaching. Our presence is taken for granted and yet denied and we are enticed into narratives which reduce us by exalting us (Holley, 1996).

Finally I believe that educational research should be influential. I want my voice to be heard and I want to share my values and persuade others about the significance of my work. I want my research to have equal status with other research in the academy and it is not useful when influential academics set themselves as the gatekeepers of what is to constitute research there (Hammersley, 1993; D'Arcy, 1994). I believe that I am committed to intervene if I think I can bring about change for the better.

Jack's position on educational research

I, Jack, hold the position, indeed it is part of my vocational commitment, that what constitutes good quality educational research will be understood as part of the process of reconstructing educational theory, educational research methodology and the epistemology of educational knowledge. Good quality educational research for me is concerned with the creation and testing of educational theory. Its quality may be judged by the extent to which it reconstitutes educational theory in the sense of developing more appropriate forms of explanation than those which exist at present for the educational development of individuals and communities. Part of the creation of new forms of explanation for the educational development of individuals concerns the epistemological issue of defining the standards of judgement which can be used to test the validity of such claims to educational knowledge. Thus the clarity of the explication and justification of such criteria, in relation to explanations for the educational development of individuals and communities, offers a way of judging the highest quality educational research.

Good quality educational research must be related to the human spirit and an aesthetic and ethic of existence. My case rests on the inclusion of spiritual, aesthetic and ethical judgements in the creation and testing of educational theory. I see this theory as being constituted by the living forms of explanation which individuals produce for their own educational development as learners in enquiries of the kind, 'How do I live my values more fully in my practice?', or 'How do I help my pupils to improve the quality of their learning?', or 'How do I improve my professional practice?'. Placing 'I' in an educational enquiry shows the engagement of a human spirit, a life-affirming spirit, in the enquiry.

The necessity of an aesthetic judgement in evaluating the quality of educational research is related to the idea of living educational theories. In producing their own educational theories, individuals give a form to their own lives in enquiries of the kind, 'How do I improve my practice?'. As artists give a form to whatever medium they are working in, educators and educational researchers are also artists in the sense that they work at giving a form to their own lives and at enabling others to give a form to theirs.

Values are intimately related to judgements as to what counts as 'educational'. I cannot distinguish something as educational without approving it. However, there is often disagreement as to which values constitute activities as 'educational'. Values can be articulated in terms such as freedom, justice, care, integrity, truth, knowledge and democracy. However, in the post-modern context it is difficult to sustain the justification of values in relation to a 'Grand Narrative' or 'Theory'. What I do in my own educational research is to attempt to embody my values in my practice and to clarify their meanings in the course of accounting, in a variety of public fora, for their emergence in enquiries of the kind, 'How do I improve my practice?'. From my perspective good educational research will embody the values which constitute the research as 'educational' and the researcher will clarify and justify these values in her or his practice.

I think good quality educational research must make a contribution to educational knowledge. For me, this assertion raises questions about the nature of educational knowledge and the question of what is the relationship between educational knowledge and other forms of knowledge. I am assuming that educational knowledge is similar to other forms of knowledge in that it can be distinguished by the forms of its explanations and the methods used to validate its claims. Educational enquiries are, in some sense, focused on what it means to live a good and productive life. This is the distinction I want to uphold and I want to see case studies by individuals showing this.

Finally, for me to acknowledge research as 'educational' I must see that it is showing its value base in a way which is life-affirming; it must be related to human beings giving a form to their own lives; it must embody such values as freedom, justice, democracy, truth and care. It must be systematic and open to public accountability with comprehensible standards of judgement for testing the claims to knowledge. In requiring that educational research embodies such values and commitments I see it as leading to a better world.

Moyra's position on educational research

Good quality educational research for me is practitioner research. It is about me changing as a result of my research and striving to live my values more consistently in my practice as an educational manager. This means that I need to identify and recognise these values, and to face up to contradictions in my practice, acting to overcome them (Whitehead, 1993:80). Educational research should include an exploration of self-knowledge and experience. I have found this is facilitated by using fictionalised forms of writing. Using story has enabled me to share and develop complex explanations that include both emotional and rational elements. I have used story with others so that we have formed a critical research community in which each of us is able to empathise with the experiences of each other, and through doing so nurture each other's thoughts to maturity (Belenky *et al.*, 1986:221). This community has provided opportunities in which we can challenge each other's thinking through dialectical critique, and require each other to face our mirror image as it is given back to us (Winter, 1989:46-55). It is through these processes that educational research has enabled me and my co-researchers to change ourselves and the situations we are researching. It is through our relationships in this research community, our 'connectedness' with each other and our interest in each other's work, that we are able to learn and change. My principles of action research are based on those of Lomax (1995a) but they have been adapted to include a greater emphasis on the self, feelings and experiences. They are:

❑   that action research is about improving practice through intervention and demands rigorous planning, observing, collecting of data, reflecting on it, replanning, and validating claims to learning;

❑   that action research is about understanding and developing our sense of ourselves, through listening, talking, sharing, and supporting;

❑   that action research can use fiction to stimulate reflection and to challenge taken for granted assumptions. Action research enables the tentative, fictional self to struggle with the 'everyday' self, and celebrate our emergence with – maybe – changed values, attitudes, beliefs, behaviours and feelings;

❏   that action research is about dialogue, collegiality and support for each other. It is about building a learning community that recognises the centrality of feelings, and the need to express these as part of the learning process;

❏   that action research is our own voyage of discovery about our lived experiences, using the literature to develop our thinking about our practices;

❏   that action research can be reported as an authentic story of our development, accessible to colleagues, and judged against the principles which have emerged during the course of our enquiry.

In search of epistemology

Epistemology is not a word that appears often in the literature on management, let alone in writings about quality in education, but it is a word associated with research, and we have focused on educational action research as the means to quality educational management. Between us we manage school pupils, prospective teachers, practising teachers and research students. Like you, if we are to turn our descriptions of our educational management practice into explanations (theories), we will do better if we understand the body of knowledge to which they will contribute. This body of knowledge, we have argued, is constituted by the 'living theories' of educators like yourselves and us. Understanding the grounds upon which this knowledge is constituted is understanding its epistemology.

> **1. If you can provide a validated account of how you have brought quality management to education through your action research, you have contributed to the creation of 'living theory'.**

Living theory is constituted by our own descriptions and explanations of our educational practice as we strive to become more effective (Whitehead, 1989). The principles we use to explain our actions come from the educational values which are embodied in our practice. These are the yardsticks against which we can measure our effectiveness. The validation of this process depends on us being able to provide convincing arguments for the importance and adequacy of our descriptions and to show their direct contribution to our explanations. This makes methodology an essential and integral part of our enquiries. Our explanations are offered in a dialogical form as a series of questions and tentative answers rather than as factual knowledge. Our explanations embrace the contradictions in our practices and as we resolve these contradictions our theories change. They are 'living' in this sense.

> Let me, Moyra, give an example from my work as a member of a secondary school's senior management team whose completed Ph.D. Pam and Jack jointly supervised. As a deputy headteacher I focused on my responsibility for staff development (Evans, 1995a; Pimenoff, 1994). This was a practical issue that I had to address in my daily life at school. I began my action research by monitoring my weekly meetings as I supported a group of teachers who wanted to improve the exam results of children in a particular subject area. In doing this I tried to apply Pam's six principles of action research (Lomax, 1995a). At the end of the first year I could demonstrate that I had substantial and valid data about the cycles of action research in which I had engaged. I was able to offer some convincing explanations about what had happened, drawing evidence from the data and sometimes refining my explanations as I shared my interpretations with critical audiences. I was beginning to develop theories about how to support teachers in school based staff development and how to deal with the ethical issues that could arise. I was also beginning to identify a new and original method for achieving my aims through my use of fictionalised writing and my encouragement of other teachers to use it (see chapter 7). By the time I submitted my thesis I could see how the whole process of my enquiry – the practical, ongoing action towards the imagined solutions, the collection of valid data to support the generation of explanations, the methodological imperatives implied in my use and adaptation of the six principles of action research, and continual testing out of my ideas against the yardstick of my educational values – contributed to my formulation of living theory (Evans, 1995b).

---

2. If you can describe and explain your practice in bringing quality management to education in relation to your own educational values you have begun to develop the explanatory principles for understanding the grounds of your own professional knowledge.

Although educational goals have been described by philosophers in their explanations of the aims of education, we prefer to work from our own values when we explain our educational practices supporting the work of educational managers, teachers and students at Kingston University, at the University of Bath, and at Denbigh School. We think that our pursuit of educational goals is about living our own personal educational values in our practice as educators. Our explanation of our practice as educational practice is based on, and is comprehensible, in terms of our values. Values are those qualities which provide meaning and purpose in our lives and which also provide the explanatory principles for why we make the judgements we do. We do not mean that values are absolute qualities that necessarily remain unchanged. An aspect of the 'living' quality of educational theory is that values are questioned, modified, clarified and sometimes changed as the research proceeds.

> For example I, Moyra, began my research with a clear conviction that the school had to help its teachers become as effective as possible. This conviction was based on clear values that children ought to have the best education and that teachers ought to get satisfaction from their work. I saw my responsibility as providing support so that teachers could develop their practice in the ways that seemed most appropriate, but still from my perspective as deputy headteacher. By the time I had submitted my Ph.D. thesis I had come to realise that the professional development of teachers depended on their own perceived needs rather than those determined by others. I was able to clarify my values to emphasise my new insight that teachers ought to be active in determining their own professional development and that their feelings and emotions should be valued in relation to this.

One of the reasons why it is particularly important to affirm the importance of personal educational values as the basis for explaining educational practices is to do with the condition called postmodernity. In all areas of social life, the certainties of the past have been challenged so that there are no longer single prescribed ways of thinking and acting. Such was the certainty of the past that 'education' was seen as a field of knowledge, to be explained by theories and research framed by the social sciences in their own value free terms. Management knowledge was similarly objectified, being usually viewed as a business practice rather than an educational practice, and judged in terms of the standards and criteria of the former rather than the latter. Yet, we believe that it is only by establishing our own value positions, testing them out with relevant others, and ensuring that we live them in practice, that we can play our part as educators, whether classroom practitioners, lecturers, subject co-ordinators, department and year heads, senior staff or inspectors and administrators.

> **3. If you are researching your action in endeavouring to bring quality management to education you have started the disciplined process towards generating knowledge about your practice.**

An understanding of quality practice cannot be separated from the means through which we define and extend the practices that constitute that quality. The research methods of social science and business provide technical links between the object and objectification of the practice, whereas in action research the means and ends are merged so that methodology and theory inter-twine in the service of practical, morally committed action which we call praxis. We are not alone in arguing this case, and other writers like Skolimowski (1992; 1994) have described the inter-connectedness of means and ends that are intimately linked and translatable into each other. Skolimowski describes a yoga or method of participation which stresses the participative, collaborative features that Pam includes in two of her six principles of action research (Lomax, 1995a) and emphasises inter-subjective understanding and empathy in much the same way that Moyra has emphasised feeling and connectedness (Evans, 1995b:91-93). He also describes a yoga of transformation, which contains advice about how we can transform our own understanding through self-reflective strategies that recognise other dimensions of the human condition besides the scientific, rational ones. This is similar to Jack's inclusion of an imagined solution in his visualisation of the action research cycles and reinforces his emphasis on the importance of spiritual and aesthetic criteria (Whitehead, 1993:69).

But we think that we have gone further than Skolimowski who is criticised for his lack of self-doubt or critical self-questioning (Parrott, 1995). In living theory, practical educational explanations are particularly powerful because they form part of the process of trying to improve the quality of professional practice; they involve researching our action as we try to bring about improvement by working to reduce the gap between our values and the practice.

> I, Jack, like to conceptualise this as my experience of the dialectic of existing as a living contradiction.
>
> I, Pam, prefer to see it as the living dilemma of having to compromise between competing value positions.
>
> I, Moyra, see it as having to clarify half formed ideas in my brain which have given rise to ill-conceived concerns and worries about my practice.

In each case, we choose not to separate method and theory or disconnect research from our educational practices. However, we recognise that this is not a simple thing to observe in the messy real world of practice (Griffiths, 1990:56). Van Manen (1995) helps clarify this messiness in his distinction between contemporaneous reflection (done during the act), retrospective reflection (done after the act) and anticipatory reflection (done before the act). He thinks that contemporaneous reflection or reflection in action (Schön, 1983) is not practical because it would lead to a split sense of self where action is inhibited. We agree with van Manen that 'the active practice of teaching is too busy to be truly reflective' (p.35) and that consciously to reflect on what one does as one acts would be to 'experience a split sense of self – a self as observed and objectified by others and a self trying to deal with situations' (p.40). This is why we would make a video record of practice, so that we can stand back and engage in retrospective reflection in order better to imagine a solution in the future (Whitehead, 1993:70,100) or we would write stories to explore the past and to imagine the future (Evans, 1995b).

---

4. If you are theorising the grounds of your own knowledge, you are developing your epistemology of your personal practice

---

We see that not all current knowledge of education is appropriate to the educational tasks at hand. We think we need professional knowledge in the form of living theory to underpin our management of schools and colleges if we are to manage better. Dewey saw practical judgements (like scientific judgements) as both intellectual and theoretical. He said 'the reflection involved in practical situations only differs in that it has a special kind of subject matter; it is concerned with the things to do or be done, judgements of a situation demanding action' (Dewey, 1916:335). We would add that values define the purpose of education and therefore are at the core of living educational theories. But the creation of living theories about educational practice can occur without our understanding the grounds of our own professional knowledge. Where we are able to theorise about the grounds of our own knowledge of our practice we have begun to develop our individual epistemologies of personal educational practices.

We think that van Manen's (1995) ideas clarify this point. He writes from a phenomenological perspective, basing his insights on his work as a teacher trainer. He has identified a phenomenology of tactful action in which he sees tact as a form of practical knowledge that becomes real in action (p.45). He argues that tact 'possesses its own epistemological structure that manifests itself first of all as a certain kind of acting: an active intentional consciousness of thoughtful human interaction' (p.43) in which practitioners act 'with the head and the heart and must feelingly know what is the appropriate thing to do' (p.33). We can associate strongly with van Manen's emphasis on the affective domain, particularly where he talks of 'a kind of practical normative intelligence that is governed by insight while relying on feeling' (p.44).

Let us recap our argument. A living theory is one that is continuously created and recreated through the validated explanations that individual managers offer of their own practices as they pursue their educational goals. These explanations are stimulated by intentional, committed action that stems from practical concerns about managing, and are reached through the analysis of careful descriptions that depend on rigorous methods of data collection and analysis. The way in which we, as individuals, understand and theorise the grounds of our personal knowledge of our professional practices, we call our epistemologies of our practices. Epistemology refers to the explanatory principles which underpin particular bodies of knowledge, what the Oxford Dictionary refers to as 'the theory of the method or grounds of knowledge'. It is by exploring the process of our own action research and reaching a metacognitive understanding of this that we are able to theorise the grounds of our own contributions to knowledge and develop our epistemologies of our own practices.

---

5. If you are making your personal epistemologies of your own practices public you are contributing to an educational epistemology of practice.

We would like to conclude our discussion of epistemology by emphasising the importance of making a contribution to public knowledge as a *profession of educators*. To do this we need to be able to theorise the grounds of professional educational knowledge so that we can distinguish it from other forms of knowledge. We argue that practitioners' individual epistemologies of their practices, once in the public domain, contribute to a new epistemology of practice that should exist alongside more traditional epistemologies. This is important because unless our view of epistemology is accepted in the academy, the forms of professional knowledge that we support are denied certain academic forms of legitimation such as higher degrees that are an important currency in our society (Whitehead and Lomax, 1987; Whitehead, 1993:79-92). We also believe that we need to be able to make a convincing case for our special claims to professional educational knowledge if we want to see 'Education' or 'Teaching' as an independent profession that is allowed to run its own business in terms of its own imperatives (Lomax, 1995b). As a profession of educators we think that we need to collaborate in order to reduce what Hargreaves calls the uncertainty of postmodernism. We need to create a 'collective professional confidence that can help teachers resist the tendency to become dependent on false scientific certainties ... by replacing them ... with the situated certainties of collective professional wisdom among particular communities of teachers' (Hargreaves, 1995:153). We see this as supporting an argument for situated epistemologies of individual practice that are validated in particular practice contexts. But we would like to take this argument further so that the validated accounts that practitioners make public of their own educational practices are seen to contribute to a dialogical community that both informs and is informed by each individual account (Lomax, 1986a; McNiff *et al.*, 1992:91-96; McNiff, 1993:71-98). The metatheory about the method or way in which this living knowledge is constituted by this knowing community is what we call an epistemology of educational practice.

Concluding reflections

We have argued that we can explain our own epistemologies of our educational management practices and that these epistemologies contribute to an educational epistemology of management practice through the kind of dialogue we have presented in this chapter and through opening this dialogue to others through its publication. We think that our own educational management practices are not only governed by principles of effectiveness, but also by special normative, ethical, aesthetic and affective considerations. We have identified a number of possible standards for judging our claims to have contributed to educational knowledge: ethical standards, standards of rigour and logic, aesthetic standards, spiritual standards and practical standards (Whitehead, 1982; Whitehead and Foster, 1984; Lomax, 1994c).

Holding ourselves accountable to these standards and to each other gives rise to the questions which take our enquiries and our practice forward. We would like to end our paper by asking you to consider whether our ideas have any significance and meaning for you and whether you would be willing to join a dialogue with us and share any insights you may have into ways of improving the quality of our management practices.

Chapter 2

Quality management is collegiate management:
improving practice in a special school

Douglas Bone

> 'I wonder what sustains you in being a head and in running a
> school if you do not have that inner belief and that inner vision,
> because it is a mighty rough mountainside that you are
> climbing and unless you have those golden dreams at the top
> (some of which you may modify, some of which you may
> never achieve), unless you have them there, it is a heavy path
> to tread if you do not know why' (West, 1993:47).

For some years, as headteacher of a special school for children with
emotional and behavioural difficulties, I have tried to build a culture of
trust and mutual understanding within which all teachers could exercise
leadership. Being seen to be living these values in school is particularly
important today because many educational values have been challenged
and destroyed. I became concerned that the collegiate values of the school,
which I believed gave the school its moral direction, were not visible in
our daily management practices. I expected my senior management staff
to encourage active participation from all members of their teams. For
example, the procedure for doing the timetable was that there was a

consultation period when all staff gave their timetable preferences. These preferences were put together in a draft and finalised at a staff meeting. I was shocked when a senior colleague was given the task of drawing up the timetable and returned it completed the next day. When challenged, she said that colleagues were not interested in being consulted! I felt that it was the senior management team's responsibility to ensure that others got interested and it was my responsibility to enable the senior staff to do this. I suspected that the values and practices of collegiality were not clear and my assumptions that they were shared were wrong. These concerns were brought to a head during a school inspection early in 1992 which highlighted the fact that some recently appointed staff were not clear about the collegiate management approach and their role in it. More seriously, the inspectors questioned the effectiveness of senior management in supporting a collegiate approach. The aim of my action research project became to clarify, share and document the values of a collegiate management practice and to improve its implementation by senior staff (including myself).

Values are beliefs that underpin the working of any organisation but are particularly important to schools, as I argue later. Values have been defined as concepts of the desirable which tend to act as motivating determinants of behaviour and some people have argued that shared values such as aesthetic, moral, strategic, personal and group values can lead to increased effectiveness (Hodgkinson, 1983; Peters, 1988; West, 1993). I agree with this, but would add that values need to be challenged and changed in line with changing needs and changing situations. I am aware of the pitfalls: the need to accommodate to conflicting values; the risk of bland, conservative, watered-down values; the danger of values becoming so internalised in a school's culture that they resist change. There is an obvious leadership role here, in promoting the generation of collected shared vision. But although my values committed me to a democratic form of school management, I became aware that my personality and my responsibility to a legal administrative role with its important dimension of accountability to the governing body (West-Burnham, 1992:71) produced a potential conflict for my practice. Yet, where the central values of the collegiate school are being lived in practice, the governing body should be part of that process. This might seem a threatening strategy but it is important to remember that one does not lose responsibility because some of it is shared with others. This is the basis of what I mean by collegiality.

Collegiality involves a process of discussion by groups of staff who share in the management of a school and are involved in setting institutional and personal goals as well as implementing them (Bush, 1986:48). The collegiate approach emphasises collaboration and teamwork, enabling each member to contribute to school decision making. When selecting staff I endeavour to explain my view of collegiality and the commitment it will need from them. I also emphasise the staff development implications. The collegiate approach can be seen as allowing staff to be involved in learning experiences every day. The flexibility it offers fits the current changing nature of education, making it easier to meet new demands. Thus collegiality can be the tool for teacher empowerment and professional enhancement. Yet collegiality is often seen as difficult by senior management because it is felt to undermine their role. This is particularly so where a member of senior staff is used to managing by position power, making decisions which they feel should be carried out because they are senior. The collegiate model means that the senior staff might have to take a side role, as particular situations demand leaders who have situational knowledge. Bush (1986:34) calls this 'an authority of expertise, where professionals possess authority arising directly from their knowledge and skills'. Stepping down from position power to accommodate this can be a very threatening experience for senior staff.

I am very conscious of the difficulties of implementing collegiality, the danger of achieving a contrived rather than a real collegiality, of using collegiality as a manipulative device rather than a way of enhancing staff autonomy (Fullan, 1992:107). The collegiate style can be cumbersome and time consuming, particularly if staff are unclear about their collegial roles. Collegiality involves staff in deciding who should do which task, and decision making can be slowed down by the search for compromise. The skill of the head and the senior team is to enable staff to find a balance between decision saturation, where staff are overloaded, and decision deprivation, where staff are not involved (Belasco and Alluto, 1972). I believe that it is important to combine power sharing with structural solutions, such as working in teams and eliminating the traditional first line manager. Peters (1988:296) suggested that teams were the 'basic organisational building blocks', and working in teams rather than individually could achieve 'enhanced focus, task orientation, innovations and individual commitment'. This flatter model of management is the collegiate model that I favour.

Action research and collegiality

Southworth has said that working towards a collegiate approach is working in the dark because so few published models are available. To me this is what made my research so interesting, that I could 'regard both leadership and collegiality as an invitation to enquiry, not as a rhetoric of conclusion' (Southworth, 1988:56). Reflecting on collegiality taught me that ownership is a key to effective participation. Similarly in research. Hopkins, in his *A Teacher's Guide to Classroom Research* (1987) has argued that if teachers are to change their practice as a result of research, research cannot be a top down activity where findings are presented by an expert. Neither can it be long and drawn out with findings that are not easy to apply in schools.

Education is changing very quickly and teachers must address new problems quickly too. Many research methods come from the social sciences and impose a disciplines framework on definitions of school issues that is different from teachers' views formed through participation in school life Although social science research leads to generalisation, it is argued that generalisation in the scientific sense is of little use to teachers for whom education is a lived experience of an uncertainty about what is worthwhile rather than a quantifiable technical operation (Bell, 1987; Gurney, 1989; Lomax, 1994d).

Action research is a means of gaining control over the environment and making sense of it. It is 'collaborative, non-hierarchical, self-managed ... sharing information, ideas and decision making' (Webb, 1991:18). It brings a boost in confidence, a feeling of self-satisfaction and an increase in corporate planning and decision making. I chose action research not only because of the limitations of traditional research but also because of my own values. I believe action research is in harmony with an enquiry geared to improving collegiate management and can contribute to both personal and institutional development.

I used the cyclical spiral of planning, action and evaluation to discipline the enquiry. I was influenced by McNiff's model where a central column reflects the main focus of enquiry and keeps the researcher on track while side spirals allow the researcher to follow up other issues (McNiff, 1988:45). This model avoids the research becoming a straitjacket on change, where a rigid plan inhibits the full exploitation of research possibilities. In fact the researcher may decide eventually to make a side spiral the main research focus.

I kept a careful record of all activities associated with the project. Monitoring action was difficult. I was unable to tape staff meetings which had to be minuted longhand but I taped most other conversations and meetings. This provided ample material but enormous problems in transcribing, filing or dealing with the data. In order to get additional feedback about how I was perceived as a leader, I used two questionnaires with staff which were relatively easy to administer but took time to collate and analyse. I also used interviews which provided excellent material and had the advantage of allowing me to delve deeper on issues. I used video only once, to record my validation meeting. It was the best method for me because I could revisit it frequently and it retained much of the quality of the original event. It was a pity I only used it once. I kept a research diary. As the research developed I honed my skills and became more adept at picking up salient points. From writing down everything verbatim, I developed the skill of making headings and developing my reflections on them later. This was still time-consuming and I was conscious of its subjectiveness, but in action research this is compensated by testing out one's interpretations with other people.

I asked three people to act as critical friends (Lomax, 1991b:108-110); one was my deputy (S), one was a member of staff (J) and the other was from outside the school, a friend who was also a business consultant (W). I selected my critical friends in order to get a range of different responses to my work. They helped me reflect on my practice and validate my research claims. W was particularly useful as I had to explain things more carefully for him as he came from outside the school and outside education.

I worked also within a support set of headteachers (Lomax, 1991b: 105-108) who were all working for an M.A. at Kingston University, and this reduced the tendency for me to feel isolated as a headteacher embarked on action research. In the early stages I did not use the group very well. I had unreal expectations and became frustrated. Through negotiation I was able to understand the group better and as a result I was able to benefit and contribute. The group met weekly to discuss work but they were also on the end of a phone for problems or reflection.

I have used a number of ways to validate my research. Validation is the process of ratifying or confirming the authenticity and reliability of research findings (Forward, 1989:34; Lomax, 1991b:110-113). In my text I have included detailed descriptions of events, comments from my diary and quotations from those involved in my action cycles. I have collected data from interviews. I have sought out the views of my support set and critical friends to enable me to compare my own perception of events with theirs. I have made my research public and subjected it to a formal validation meeting which was attended by my tutor from Kingston University, two members of my support set, my three critical friends and two teachers about to enrol for the second year of the M.A. As a result of this meeting I gained an enhanced understanding of my research and was able to identify a way forward to presenting a dissertation successfully (Bone, 1993).

The aim of the enquiry

The aim of my research was to improve the practice of the collegial management that we as a school espoused in theory; to close the gap between theory and practice and thus to resolve the living contradiction of my practice. I wanted a situation in which values of collegiality were shared and clear and could be seen in action between staff and between staff and pupils. I knew that colleagues had to be convinced that they would benefit from giving support to my research. This had to be made clear and was my first challenge. I was looking to improve the way the whole school operated. I believed that I would know when the situation had improved by an increase in staff participation in decision making. To demonstrate that improvement had occurred I would need to show changes in people's actions. Eventually I would hope to make claims about what I had achieved with evidence to support them.

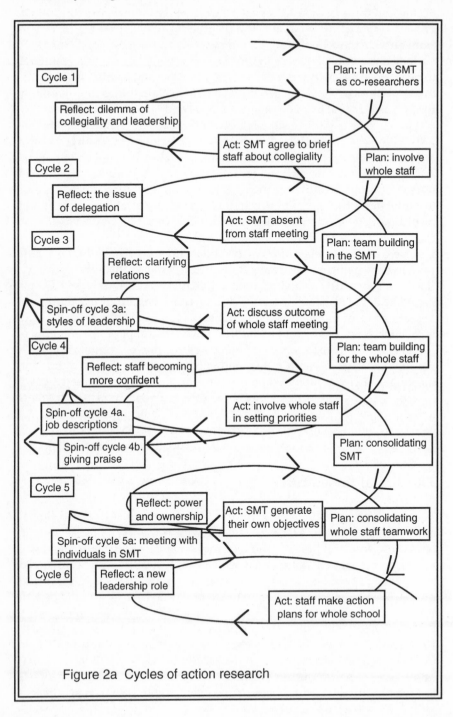

Figure 2a Cycles of action research

My main cycles of action research cover a period from January to August 1993. Before that I spent a term of reconnaissance in which I learned about action research and formulated my early plans. Figure 2a summarises the six main cycles of action research and a number of spin-off cycles. For each cycle I devised a plan, recorded what happened and tested my explanation in discussions with others. The cycles blended into each other, as each was formed as the result of changes brought about by observations of previous action. The first cycle was initiated by me without much consultation. As I moved through the research, other people's perspectives on issues appeared: support set, critical friends, colleagues and tutor. Their perceptions contributed to changes of plan and changes in my understanding of what happened. This was following the particular model of action research within which I was working at Kingston University and has been described elsewhere (Lomax, 1994a).

Cycle 1
Involving the SMT as co-researchers

I began my first cycle of action research in January 1993 at one of my weekly meetings with my senior management team which took place on a Monday morning. My intention at that first meeting was to outline my research and establish with my colleagues a shared perspective on the values of collegiality. There were three members of the team besides myself: my deputy (S), the senior teacher in the primary department (C) and the senior teacher in the secondary department (B).

Bell (1987:42) says that teachers, administrators, parents and keepers of documents need to be convinced of the researcher's integrity and the value of their research before they decide whether or not to cooperate; and that participants want to see some pay-off for giving access. At the meeting I gave the SMT as much information about action research as possible. I discussed collegiality and values and asked for colleagues' views about how we could involve staff in a discussion of values. I outlined a plan for a full staff meeting in which we could demonstrate in our practice that we were acting collegially. The team appeared to me to be enthusiastic and the two senior teachers agreed to take the lead in presenting key aspects of our plan to the rest of the staff.

After the meeting I had a conversation with S about how it had gone. She said, 'It went well; nice to see C so positive ... We are clear on what we have to do.' She also challenged me for being too directive. She said I had led the discussion a lot of the time and I should have encouraged others to participate more; after all, that was the point of my research.

Reflection 1
The dilemma of collegiality and leadership

Although I recognised that I needed others to participate, I also felt that as the headteacher I should take the lead. This has proved to be an ongoing dilemma for me and was highlighted by the conversation I had with S following that first meeting of the senior management team. How much should I lead? I did not want to dominate that first meeting as C would sit back. How do I achieve a balance between my values about collegial management and my need to take control? Tannenbaum and Schmidt (1991:26) identify this dilemma of leadership as a common problem for modern managers who often '... are not sure how to behave. There are times when they are torn between exerting strong leadership and permissive leadership ... they are not sure when group decision is really appropriate or when holding a staff meeting serves merely as a device for avoiding their own decision-making responsibility'.

I had started my action research defensively, as a reaction to a school inspection which questioned the effectiveness of the senior managers at my school in supporting a collegiate approach to managing the school. The inspectors had suggested that we

'... review the role of the SMT in the collegiate model and consider whether the role needs to change so that it is not perceived to be so critically dependent on staffing at this level. The school needs to be sure that the school needs to operate itself in a collegiate manner, is mutually supportive and does not have expectations placed upon itself that mitigate against collegiality by shifting the focus of responsibility away from others towards itself' (Inspection Report, 1992) (school remains anonymous: Editor).

I had taken the inspectors' comments as being a criticism of collegiality and was unable to answer them at that time. It was only during the process of my research that I came to understand these dilemmas more fully. For example, at my validation meeting in June 1993 a member of the panel said: 'Have you asked yourself why you have more experienced people? Is it usually because they are more along the route to what you are trying to do? Having more senior people is not necessarily a contradiction to collegiality. Is it that they might be more expert and were able to help newer people?' This exchange helped me to formulate a clearer view of management in the collegiate approach and relate what the inspectors had meant to a comment made by Fiddler and Bowles (1991:13), that 'senior managers by virtue of their position will typically have access to more and better information about the future than their colleagues, not all of which are in a position to share'.

A more thorough evaluation of the first SMT meeting, and more careful reflection on the comments of my deputy headteacher might also have highlighted the contradiction between the way I saw myself as a leader and my values about collegiality. The term 'living contradiction' comes from the work of Whitehead (1993:70) who explains that an incentive for teachers to improve their educational practices is their recognition that they do not live out their values fully in their practice. Talking about action research at a Conference at Kingston University in July 1993, Whitehead said, 'There are so many things that are changing in education at the moment, that we need to go back to the values we hold dear. We must try to keep them.' This was refreshing to hear as I had interpreted the inspection report as a challenge to my values about collegiality. Writing my values down gave me clarity and strength but it also made me reflect on why I held them and how far I was prepared to go to protect them. Discussing these values and making them public provided more clarity. As a result of the re-evaluation of my values in my action research I became more confident in my adoption of the collegiate approach, despite being aware of myself and others in the school as living contradictions. If professional values are strong and public they can help institutions to resist ill-thought-out change. I perceived a clash between my values and those of the inspectors. This can be a problem when your innovation is beyond the understanding of those who have to judge and this will become more of a problem with the new inspection. However, it is also important to take criticism seriously. I came to realise how important it is to be open and to evaluate one's practice and reassess one's values in the light of different points of view. One member of staff whose views I sought later in the research added a further dimension to what the inspectors had said. She spoke about staff expectations about the SMT. What could the SMT offer other staff? How would they justify their more senior position? Her view was that although staff appreciated the collegiate way of working and wanted to play a part in school decision making, they also looked to senior staff for support and expertise. She thought that there needed to be a balance between support and autonomy *(interview with member of staff)*.

At this time I made the first of a series of three drawings in which I tried to visualise my action research. This was partly because I was dissatisfied with the cyclical models of action research found in the text books and my support set, at the instigation of the tutor, were experimenting with different ways of representing their work. Some of this experimentation has since been described in a paper by Lomax and Parker (1995). My first drawing shows my research as a spiral of actions with myself as the column at the centre (see Figure 2b). This was intended to indicate my full involvement in the cycle as I outlined my research to colleagues and put some of my initial plans into action.

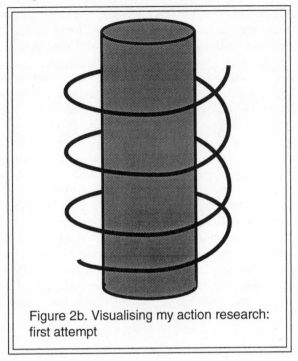

Figure 2b. Visualising my action research: first attempt

Cycle 2
Drawing the whole staff into the project

At my school, staff meetings follow a three week sequence of departmental meetings, curriculum meetings and whole staff meetings and involve all the teaching and non-teaching staff. The second cycle of action research was to introduce the idea of collegiality at a whole staff meeting and to get staff to commit themselves to taking part in the research. I also wanted staff to see the SMT working as a team. My intention was to introduce my research and to get the two senior teachers to present discussion papers on values and collegiality as had been agreed. This was to be followed by staff discussion of three open questions. These questions had been prepared by me, modified after consultation with my support group, and agreed by the SMT. The questions were:

1. What are the values which underpin the school's collegiate model?
2. Where are there examples of the collegiate approach in practice in the school ?
3. Where are there examples of the collegiate model not working in the school?

In the event, both colleagues who were to present papers were absent through illness. I went ahead with the meeting. Staff were split into pairs for an initial discussion of the questions and then formed larger groups to agree their feedback in a plenary. The final statements were recorded for further discussion at a later date. I selected this activity as I thought it would encourage participation. I was pleased with the result and with the very lively exchanges in each of the groups. I was disappointed with the two members of the SMT who were missing. I saw this as a missed opportunity, but I felt the meeting had achieved its aims.

Follow-up discussion about the staff meeting with S and J, my school-based critical friends, confirmed my evaluation of events, but W, my external critical friend was more challenging. Why had I gone ahead with the meeting when key personnel were missing? Had I resorted to the role of solitary hero leader and undermined the collegial authority of my senior managers? Had I helped to reinforce a negative view of the senior staff amongst some of the other staff? Had I considered other reasons why the two senior members of staff had not attended? Had they got the confidence and skills to do the job I gave them? Had I helped them prepare sufficiently? Were they clear about what was expected?

Reflection 2
The issue of delegation

The response of W came as a big shock. I had acted precipitously without sufficient reflection. I had succeeded in getting the staff to discuss collegiality and come to their own view of what it meant, but I had not thought carefully enough about involving my senior staff. I would have to reflect more on the way I was acting and challenge my own assumptions. I considered a point made by Tannenbaum and Schmidt (1991:30), that '..to provide the individual or the group with greater freedom than they are ready for at any given time may very well tend to generate anxieties and therefore inhibit rather than facilitate the attainment of the desired objectives'. Had this been the case at my initial meeting with the senior staff? Had I failed to recognise their anxiety about the changes I was trying to implement? Or had my actions been even less democratic than that? Was I guilty of what Vulliamy and Webb (1991:233) describe, where '...in extreme forms, research could merely become a manipulative device to justify and implement pre-specified changes with little or no modification to existing plans or increased understanding of the issues'?

At that time I also shared my concerns with my support set, and although their gentle criticism of the autocratic style and language with which I expressed my plans to help senior staff was lost on me at the time, I did recognise that the way I had represented my research in my initial visualisation showed a stark separation between myself and the very colleagues with whom I was trying to foster more collegial relationships. This led me to revise the initial drawing (Figure 2c) so that the central column (representing me) and the circling spiral of action (representing my effort to forge collegiality) was linked by arrows. Because I had begun to see negotiation as particularly important (and problematic), these arrows were depicted with two heads so that they could be seen to go backwards and forwards between the central column and the encircling spiral. This drawing externalised my increased awareness of the need to focus on my relations with staff, particularly on delegation, and this awareness was clearly related to conversations that we were having about action research.

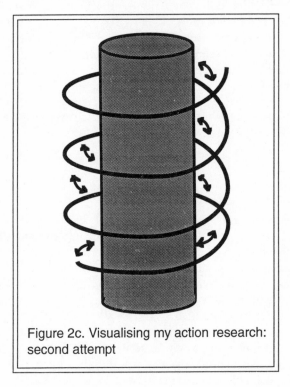

Figure 2c. Visualising my action research: second attempt

I attempted to broaden my perspective by looking at the issue of delegation in more detail. Even where collegiality does not operate, there is a need for decisions to be delegated as the role of headteacher grows. Fiddler and Bowles (1991:12) point to 'a general agreement that local management of schools will require greater involvement of a wider range of staff. The way it is suggested that this will be done is through the wider use of delegation'. This is quite a cynical view of delegation, in that the reason given is to do with lessening the head's workload. To me delegation is much more than that. A better reason for delegating can be found in the dictionary definition of 'entrusting authority to a deputy' and the view of Trethowan (1985:2) that delegation can 'develop skills of the staff, so making them more effective and improving their self-esteem and promotability'. I was to find out that poor delegation can be frustrating and undermine staff confidence as managers struggle to come to terms with a poorly defined task. It is wrong for a head to say to staff, 'Here is a task; now get on with it' and then sit back waiting for results, which was my approach in the early part of my study. Delegation is also about the head's confidence in colleagues. It is a vote of confidence. Accountability cannot be delegated; therefore there is a need for good communication when tasks are delegated. This should not mean constant checking-up. Others work in different ways and often take longer to carry out a task the leader could do much quicker. This is something I was aware of in my SMT. At first I would check progress frequently, but as I became more confident I became prepared to let go, making myself available if consultation was needed. This is in line with points made by West-Burnham (1992:112) that '... if responsibility and authority are effectively delegated then ownership is created; the job becomes a real one rather than the dumping of chores' and Nicholson (1992:44) that 'delegation should be of benefit to you and your people. You are released for other, high level work, and they receive an opportunity to develop themselves'.

As my research progressed I was influenced by Trethowan's three 'A's' of delegation to develop my own checklist. Trethowan's list included:

1. Area of responsibility clearly defined.
2. Authority to carry out the job.
3. Accountability with absolute certainty (Trethowan, 1989:3).

My check list had 5 elements:

1. that the task is clearly defined;
2. that the person who is carrying it out knows exactly what is expected of them;
3. that the person carrying out the task has the ability or training to carry out the task;
4. that I will provide the necessary support;
5. that deadlines and reviews are agreed.

Cycle 3
Second meeting of the SMT

My next action was to plan my next meeting with the SMT in which I intended to report on the staff meeting and show senior colleagues the statements about collegiality produced by the staff which I had collated and photocopied. My intention at this meeting was to retrieve some of the mistakes I saw myself as having made in the initial meeting about collegiality. I anticipated that the meeting could be difficult due to colleagues feeling uncomfortable and expecting me to be angry about being let down at the staff meeting. I was determined to practise the supportive style of leadership implied in collegiality. I needed to establish the value of support within the SMT and this meant changing my own behaviour which could be autocratic. I had discussed this with my critical friends and reached the conclusion that consolidation rather than conflict was needed if I was to get senior staff involved in my plans.

At the meeting the two senior staff seemed defensive. I apologised for going ahead with the staff meeting without them. We looked at the statements about collegiality produced by the staff, some of which were critical of senior management: 'Lack of feedback from the SMT', 'The SMT not acting in a collegiate way', 'The SMT do not have a clear role'. These negative statements were directed at the SMT collectively, enabling us to absorb them as a team rather than take them on as individuals. At this point I did not think we were ready to consider individual criticism. I encouraged discussion by asking questions. There were some long pauses but I was aware that this could happen and was prepared to wait.

At a later discussion, my critical friend, S, said the senior management meeting had gone well and that I had been less dominating. She thought our two colleagues had looked relaxed and confident. Only on the odd occasion had they reacted as if threatened. We had shared a common task in discussing staff statements on collegiality and made plans for further action. Adair (1984:129) has explained the importance of this: 'The common task provides opportunity for developing a sense of achievement, gaining status and recognition, while the group opens the door to social needs being met'. By showing that I was prepared to publish staff criticism, by being open to criticism and by using criticism as a way forward, I was setting an example. My critical friend, W, said that in order to get people to believe in open management one would need continually to reinforce that point. It was also necessary eventually for all members of the SMT to show that example.

Reflection 3
Clarifying relationships

Action research with its need to reflect, to seek feedback from critical friends and support set, helped me to challenge some of my implicit assumptions. Working in my support set, I had been encouraged to think through this meeting and imagine possible outcomes. Our combined imaginations were much more effective than my own more limited thoughts would have been. Fiddler and Bowles (1991:13) reinforce this insight: 'senior managers are prone to assume that they know more than the rank and file merely because they are senior managers. After all, is this not the reason for their selection and promotion?'

My headteachers' support set was an invaluable source of support and encouragement at this time. Many of the problems I was having with the SMT were mirrored in my early experience of the support set when I had written in my diary that it was not functioning properly. I came to understand, through discussion with another member of the set, that this was due to my own unrealistic expectations. I learnt from this that it is better to be open if you are not satisfied. The group will not improve on its own if conflict is hidden. Discussion of difficulties and expectations provides an opportunity to investigate assumptions and dispel misunderstandings. I was also made aware that I could dominate support set meetings because I had such definite views of what I wanted to achieve. I rushed the meetings to achieve my targets. I learned that I would have to slow down to benefit the group and get benefit from it. The support set were very good at keeping me to this target.

Having a vision and wanting to get on with it is only one aspect of good leadership. Kelly (1991:89) added the need for 'interpersonal skills to achieve consensus, the verbal capacity to communicate enthusiasm to large and diverse groups of individuals, the organisational talent to co-ordinate disparate efforts'. Kotter (1990) writing on leadership in *The Independent* said there are three prerequisites for bringing about change. 'First, the person leading has to set a direction or vision; then they have to get everyone lined up to go in that direction together; and then they have to inspire them and energise them enough, to get them from here to there'. He also argued that it is leadership rather than management that makes things happen. On reflection, I concluded that I had been strong on management but insufficiently assertive as a leader. I had 'done things right' but not always 'done the right things'; I had 'followed a path' but not necessarily 'found the path'; and I had promoted the idea of 'being taught by the organisation' rather than 'learning from the organisation' (West-Burnham, 1990:74).

I believe that as a result of my research I personally moved away from the solitary hero leader towards a more co-operative style of management, although I also recognised my responsibility to provide clear leadership. At times I found this difficult as I did not want to inhibit the developing collegiate responsibilities that my senior colleagues had taken on. Early in the research, my expectations were unclear and I vacillated between standing back and giving little direction then moving too quickly because I thought we were not progressing fast enough. I was to learn that some staff need time for reflection and time to make their contribution. I believed that staff were capable of producing solutions to problems and I had confidence in their technical expertise, but I did not always make my expectations clear and I did not help staff gain the confidence needed to tackle their tasks successfully. Kelly (1991:84) suggested that this can result in 'alienated followers ... critical and independent in their thinking but passive in carrying out their role ... Often cynical, they tend to sink gradually into disgruntled acquiescence, seldom openly opposing a leader's efforts'.

Spin-off Cycle 3a
Examining leadership style

At the end of the meeting reported in cycle 3 I asked colleagues if they would complete a questionnaire to give me feedback about my own leadership style. I was delighted with the response when one of the senior teachers suggested that we all should do this and that they should also ask staff in their teams to do it for them. All agreed that it was a good idea. This seemed to indicate the growing confidence of the team and their willingness to take a serious part in my research plans. C commented: 'That is living your values if staff can see we are undergoing a review from which we should all benefit ... let's face it - they have been let down by the past SMT ... we have to re-establish credibility.'

Company worker	Capable of converting plans into actions, working systematically and efficiently: a stable, controlled member of the team.
Shaper	Pushes the team towards action, sets objectives and looks for outcomes: dominant, extrovert and anxious.
Plant	Innovates, generates new ideas and approaches, problem solver: dominant, intelligent and introvert.
Resource investigator	The team contact with the environment, generates ideas and resources: intelligent, stable and introvert.
Monitor evaluator	Analyses problems and evaluates contributions: intelligent, stable and introvert.
Team worker	Supports and reinforces, improves communication, fosters team spirit: stable, extrovert and flexible.
Complete finisher	Ensures attention to detail, maintains schedules: anxious and introvert.
Chairman	Controls and makes the best use of the team, is able to balance contributions towards an objective: stable and dominant.

Figure 2d. Characteristics of team members (From Belbin, 1995)

The instrument that I chose was Belbin's (1985) self-analysis inventory. It was reputed to provide some indication of a person's strengths and weaknesses as a member of a management team. It is based on a model of eight roles which were thought to be necessary for a successful team (see Figure 2d). In smaller teams, such as the SMT, members would have to play more than one role to cover all the tasks that had to be covered. Belbin believed that the use of his self-analysis inventory could help diagnose why teams were being successful or not. The inventory was not designed specifically for education.

When we eventually analysed the results I was surprised that I did not come out as a Chairman, which I expected, but as a Shaper first and in a secondary role as a Resource Investigator. This same result appeared in both my self-assessment and in the returns of all members of staff except one. The other three members of the SMT came out first as Company Workers, with secondary roles of Chairman, Shaper and Team Worker. It appeared that we were short of a Plant, a Monitor Evaluator and a Completer Finisher.

I was concerned that the predominance of company worker behaviour was limiting and showed a lack of willingness to take on responsibility. My support group thought that this could be the case and one suggested I look at the behaviour of the missing types to see if it was possible to develop the key skills in the SMT. As a result of this I correlated the types of behaviour from the three missing types and discussed these with the SMT. Some were seen as so essential that it was agreed that we would bear them in mind throughout our dealings. This was in line with the advice that 'You need to sit down together and identify any obvious gaps in the management team as it is currently constituted' and 'As long as you are aware that you lack certain management team strengths, then you can all be on your mettle to try to compensate for that known weakness' (Hellawell, 1992:20). This particular exercise alerted me to the danger of building a management team in my own image and gave me further fodder for reflection about how collegiate management might look.

W thought it may be that I had sold *my vision* so well that staff saw their responsibility as converting my plans into action. My suspicion was that it was my own behaviour that was inhibiting the SMT from taking more initiative. W suggested that I try another questionnaire focusing on how I influence people. I used a Selling and Influence Style Questionnaire (Sundridge Management Centre) which I completed for myself and asked all staff to complete for me. I explained the reason for the questionnaire and that I hoped they would all benefit from the result which I would publish for them to discuss. I considered this another example of me living my values. I also felt that I was leading by example as I was demonstrating that I was prepared to examine my own practice in order to improve it.

The inventory has a number of questions. The answers are scored and marked onto a master sheet which puts them into the four styles and gives a score. These styles are described in Figure 2e. The score is then transferred onto a percentile score made up from a sample of several hundred British and American middle managers. I scored on the 67th percentile for assertive persuasion, the 74th percentile for reward and punishment, the 82nd percentile for participation and trust, and the 93rd percentile for common vision. I also plotted staff views of my behaviour and found that their perception was similar to mine. It is necessary on occasion for a leader to use all styles but as someone who values collegiality, I was glad that mine was predominantly participation and trust and common vision.

Style	Characteristics	Individual behaviour
Assertive Persuasion	This style is characterised by use of pressures and incentives to control behaviour of others.	Forward with ideas, not afraid to stick their neck out. Submit ideas to the test. Ingenious in marshalling evidence. Persistent and energetic. Highly verbal. Enjoys argument.
Reward and Punishment	This style is characterised by use of pressures and incentives to control behaviour of others	Go out of their way to let people know what they want, expect or require of them and what standards they will be judging them by. Follow up actions with negative or positive incentives.
Participation and Trust	This style is characterised by the involvement of others in decision making or problem solving processes.	Tend to listen actively, draw out contributions showing understanding and appreciation when contributions are forthcoming. Willing to delegate. Lead by example to develop openness and trust.
Common Vision	This style is characterised by involving, identifying and articulating a common or shared vision. It involves mobilising the energy and resources of others.	Ability to see and articulate to others the exciting possibilities which exist in an idea or project and to project these to others. Make a better future for all.

Figure 2e. Influence and selling style inventory
(Sunbridge Management Centre)

I concluded this cycle by discussing the outcome of the questionnaire with both W and the SMT. Making myself 'go public' in this led to further clarification of my thinking. This is a strategy I use in many situations now, almost going through an imagined performance. The response from the SMT was very positive. The inventory brought up a number of issues that may not have come up without it. We ended up discussing how each of us behaved and each member took away a copy of the behaviours.

Cycle 4
Whole staff meeting to prioritise ideas on collegiate practice

The fourth cycle was a meeting in which staff, excluding the SMT, were asked to work together to discuss and prioritise issues raised at the last meeting. The SMT had decided not to participate in this activity so as not to inhibit open and free discussion. The main aim of cycle 4 was to help staff develop their ideas on collegiality, but my sub-agenda was to try and foster team building, what Murgatroyd and Morgan (1993:144) called trust and mutuality. They suggested 'what binds the team is its sense of responsibility both for the process it is using for the task and the trust the individual members have in each other's skills, judgement and knowledge'. For the staff meeting I provided a collated list of all the statements that had emerged from the previous session on collegiality. The idea was for staff to prioritise these statements. They were to use the method of Snowball groups described by Fiddler and Bowles (1991:16) in which groups progressively combine and the task at each re-grouping becomes increasingly sophisticated or involves the elimination of alternatives. At the end of the snowball activity staff were asked to complete a proforma individually. I also asked J about the meeting and she gave very positive feedback. She said, 'This activity was useful as it made us think. It helped clarify our thinking. I found it threatening at first but I think we should use it more often.' I was pleased that J was beginning to contribute more to the research as the study went on. I did wonder about how honest she could be, given that I was the headteacher, but I tried to encourage her to be as objective as possible by showing that I valued her honest views and by questioning her feedback if it seemed less critical than it could have been.

Spin-off Cycle 4a
Job descriptions for the SMT

Cycle 4a took advantage of the space provided while the rest of the staff were engaged in the team building activity for a meeting of the SMT to sort out our job descriptions and work on a position statement on how we felt we should be held to account for collegiate working from the point of view of management values and action. This was the result of a remark by one of my critical friends who had queried whether staff were clear about the role of the SMT. It occurred to me that the SMT were not clear about their own roles.

I felt that the meeting was very productive. The SMT job descriptions were produced and later made available to all colleagues. I hoped that this would demonstrate our commitment to openness. It also became a prelude to job descriptions generally, with senior staff working with other teachers to help them with their job descriptions which helped alleviate some of the potential anxiety they might have felt about producing these themselves.

I had been careful to involve senior staff in this activity in such a way that they had confidence in their ability to carry it through. It was important that they had undergone the process themselves and that we had discussed our strategies for helping other colleagues carefully. By circulating our own job descriptions we hoped we had demonstrated our values of participation and openness. Comments from both school-based critical friends were positive regarding the published SMT job descriptions. A member of staff was reported as saying, 'I feel more able to question the job of the SMT, without worrying about hurting feelings or getting stick.' By working with staff to help them produce their own job descriptions, and making an effort to negotiate rather than impose ideas, I hoped that they would experience the SMT practising collegial leadership. Staff comments about the SMT, both solicited and volunteered, supported this view, suggesting that more than one member of staff had observed and commented on the fact that the SMT seemed less defensive and more open than previously. A particularly vocal colleague was reported as saying, 'I do not mind that approach to job descriptions'.

Reflection 4a
Recording progress

I was becoming more confident in the individuals and the group. Tannenbaum and Schmidt (1991:30) advise, 'before turning decision making responsibility over to a subordinate group, the boss should consider how effectively its members work together as a unit'. I felt able to give them more responsibility. My diary notes show that I felt the SMT seemed more in control. We were also becoming clearer about each other's expectations. This had been greatly helped by having published job descriptions and also the process of arriving at them through negotiation. I felt we were on the way to establishing trust and mutuality and I took the opportunity to praise them for their efforts.

Spin-off cycle 4b
Giving praise

One of my concerns at the start of the research was the apparent reluctance of senior staff to drop into colleagues' classrooms for informal discussion, an activity that I think is very important to the sort of leadership I wanted to implement. I favour what Nicholson (1992:48) has called 'management by walking about' (MBWA). A useful article clarified my thinking on the difference between management and leadership: 'Management controls people by pushing them in the right direction; leadership motivates them by satisfying basic human need' (Kotter, 1991:7). I decided that praise and recognition were basic human needs that I had been neglecting, as do many senior staff. I decided to set a target for praise at three a day. I followed the advice of my critical friend, W, who suggested I record who was receiving praise and how often. This gave more direction to my management by walking about. It had become MBWA with purpose, a style I am now firmly committed to. The praise record gave me a structured insight on the way that staff were working and also provided me with a window on my leadership and management role.

Cycle 5
Targets for SMT action

The agenda for the SMT meeting which was the basis of cycle 5 included a discussion of what action to take in response to the prioritised lists made by staff at the previous whole staff meeting. This was a difficult task and we agonised over solutions until one of the SMT suggested that the task should be given back to the staff: 'We have stated that we want to improve staff problem solving; here is a chance.' Once this solution was agreed the meeting went ahead smoothly and we were able to arrive at some long term and short term targets for our own action. These included:

(a) Short term objectives

- ❏ meetings to start and finish on time
- ❏ SMT meetings to feed back to staff teams on Tuesday mornings
- ❏ timetable alterations will be open to discussion whenever possible
- ❏ SMT will complete all job descriptions
- ❏ a working party will be organised to look at the induction of new staff

(b) Long term objectives

❏   achieve a climate where people feel they can open up and be critical

❏   establish channels of communication to assist people in saying what they think

❏   restructure morning staff meetings so that SMT members can rotate

❏   involve staff in finding alternative strategies and problem solving approaches

❏   review our responsibilities in relation to primary/ secondary departments

These objectives were generated by the team rather than imposed by me, although they were very close to my own list, made before the meeting when I was thinking about the issues. We also made an action plan to share with other staff. Some items could be acted on immediately. C suggested we involve others in small working parties to tackle some of the issues. B suggested we set performance indicators and tackle some tasks immediately.

Members of the SMT were making positive contributions. I had tried hard to reinforce, question and support ideas as I felt appropriate. This had not been the case in earlier meetings which I had dominated. In discussing how this meeting had gone, S said I had not dominated the meeting but had been very supportive and had encouraged staff with non-verbal cues and comments. Later I followed this up with the two other members of the SMT. B commented that I had always set the tempo for meetings and they had previously followed, but now I was taking more of a back seat. I was not sure that I was taking a back seat, but felt that I was just more able to let people express themselves and I made an effort actively to encourage them. I also asked C how she felt about her work. C said, 'I feel I have a much clearer role and I am happy to be held to account for that. Before staff had unfair expectations of me.' She added, 'Staff can see we are pulling together; it's not just you and the deputy.' She took this opportunity to chat about how she was trying to implement collegiality in her team and to ask for my views. I made an effort to be very positive (caught being good?) and she laughed and said, 'I have to do that as well!'

My diary of this time notes my growing satisfaction about the team and C in particular, who had become very positive. Was this because the team had been allowed to succeed publicly? Other staff had commented on changes in the SMT. Could I maintain this so that expectations of success became self-fulfilling prophesies? Adair (1984:131) quotes Emerson's comment: 'Trust men and they will be true to you. Treat them greatly and they will show themselves great'. This appeared to be happening in the team. I felt that it was the change in my own behaviour which had led to this. As I trusted staff more and was able to delegate better, staff rose to the task. The fact that they could manage without me at first was a little disconcerting, but it freed me and gave the staff satisfaction and I appreciated that this was what I was working for.

About this time I also spoke to J, who observed that the SMT seemed more of a team and were all working with more purpose. She said, 'This could be due to you developing a more up front style of leadership.' This seemed to me to be a contradiction as I felt that I had become less up front in order to adopt a more collegiate approach. I discussed this with a member of my support set who suggested that what could be happening was that my role was becoming more distinguishable from the rest of the SMT as they settled into roles. I noted in my diary my feelings of becoming less central. I was pleased but at the same time a little reluctant to let go.

Reflection 5
Power and ownership

Throughout the research the issue of ownership had been prominent. The decision to involve the whole staff in formulating an action plan for the school was an important step forward in achieving a more collegiate approach to school management. It was crucial that the suggestion came from a member of the SMT who had demonstrated how our espoused values could be lived in action and who was relinquishing ownership to enable others to become involved. This could be viewed as a shared task, not a delegated task, as the member of the SMT would be a participant in the whole school discussion at which action plans were to be made. W commented: 'This is an example of increased confidence. This sort of behaviour is supporting the building of teams. The SMT feel more confident and this is reflected in them sharing with others. You never have so much power as when you are able to give it away!'

It seemed to me that this particular episode mirrored my own situation in that as I became more confident in the SMT, they became more confident in the staff and as a result felt less threatened. In the early stages of the project I had held up progress because I feared letting go. An early example of this, suggested by W, was when I proved I was able to run the early meeting without the rest of the SMT. I discussed these developments with S who suggested that we had succeeded in establishing an appropriate climate (one of our targets). This I thought was 'where individuals and teams are encouraged to take risks, where constructive conflict and debate are seen as healthy and delegation and self-evaluation are seen as the norm' (Fiddler and Bowles, 1991:14).

Spin-off cycle 5a
Formalising individual meetings

The SMT were more reflective in meetings but were also more open in 'casual chats'. One member made an effort to see me each morning to chat over issues. The discussions were very open and frank and covered many areas of concern for the person. When I discussed this with W, he said, 'All members of staff would benefit from a formalised meeting with you, once every half term. Both you and the staff would benefit.' My support set wondered about the practicalities of a busy head doing this but I was able to convince them by showing how we would benefit. It was a question of priorities. I believe the most valuable gift you can give anyone is time. I have initiated a half termly meeting plan but I am also looking to encourage other SMT members to meet the staff they are directly responsible for.

Cycle 6
Whole staff finalising action plans

This was the last cycle of action research and was to involve the whole staff in coming up with an action plan to move the school to becoming a more collegial organisation. It followed directly from their work in cycle 2 where they identified areas of concern and in cycle 4 where they prioritised these areas. The fact that staff were involved in this way was directly related to my success in working with the senior management team who had initiated the suggestion that the whole staff should be involved in the action planning. We had identified a problem through an exercise and would ask the staff to reflect on the problem and to try to come up with solutions. This could have two benefits: an improvement in the quality of the resulting decisions and an improvement in motivation and commitment of those involved. It could also help develop staff in their problem solving.

The plan for the session was similar to that used for earlier sessions. Staff were split into pairs and we followed the snowball method. The groups settled quickly to the task, which was to discuss how the prioritised lists could be implemented. They had adopted a positive attitude to the work and seemed to enjoy it. They were arguing for their points but were also listening to others' points of view and coming to an agreement. The results of the activity were evidence that the staff had a clear perception of the SMT role and within that could make realistic suggestions about the way forward to developing collegiality further.

Reflection 6
The final cycle?

Often leadership is defined as the process of influencing group behaviour towards a common goal (West and Ainscow, 1991:29). I would take this definition further. I see leadership as the process of influencing and being influenced by a group towards goals which they have been involved in setting. S saw this as a continuum along which I should move in response to the needs of the situation. She thought that I needed to learn to be flexible in deciding my position on this continuum at any given time.

Completing cycle 6 brought me to an important stage in my enquiry, one where I felt confident that I could support a number of claims about improving the quality of relationships amongst the teachers in my school. I saw this as a stage in an ongoing enquiry which at a future date would influence what went on in the classrooms of the school and through that the future of the pupils who attended the school.

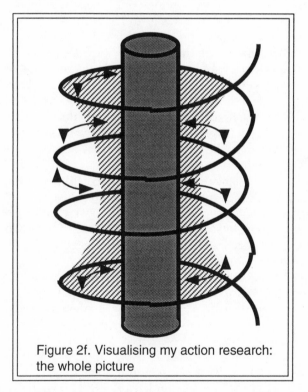

Figure 2f. Visualising my action research: the whole picture

I was also able to rethink the earlier drawings I had made to represent my research. In my final drawing (Figure 2f) the central column was replaced by an hourglass shaped figure which was connected to the circling spiral by arrows. The drawing was intended as an overview of the whole project, to show particularly how my relationship with my colleagues had changed during the period of the research. At the bottom of the figure the hourglass touches the circling spiral to depict the way in which in the early part of the research I had directed events without much negotiation. The middle of the figure depicts my attempt to withdraw from a dominant role so as to support colleagues taking more responsibility for managing the school. At the top of the drawing the hourglass again meets the encircling spiral but this time to show myself as a member of a collegiate team. In this final stage my role had become fully absorbed as I became a participant in the action rather than a leader of it.

Conclusion

This account has described and explained how I used action research to help me develop a collegiate management style in the school and encourage the SMT to involve staff fully. In completing six main action cycles and a number of spin-off cycles I can claim to have improved the quality of management in my school.

I have reviewed the values that underpin the collegiate approach with the SMT and we have worked with the rest of the staff to determine how best to achieve these. This has led to a raising of the profile of the collegiate approach and increased the awareness of the whole staff about the way collegiality can be practised. This means that the values and intentions of the school as a collegiate organisation can be made public more easily than was the case at the time of the school inspection. If a school's values are not clear, then they are open to misinterpretation and this can have dire consequences when change is so easily imposed from outside. It is also crucial to review values periodically. Once they become part of the culture of the school they can become hidden resistors to change. This is the dilemma for an innovator, 'the need to jettison the status quo for the sake of innovation. The very values on which a school prides itself may be a hindrance to moving forward' (Ryan, 1992:261).

The school has benefited from my research. Leadership in the collegiate approach aims to bring about a collaborative ethic through teams working together and redefining their purpose. The implementation of a more collegiate approach has given the SMT and other staff added motivation and an enhanced self image. The SMT have published their aims and job descriptions which have led to staff expecting the SMT to work in a collegiate manner. The process of identifying aims has gelled the staff into teams and given the SMT more confidence. As SMT have become clearer about their roles, they have functioned more effectively and have taken on more responsibility. As the staff have become clearer of the role of the SMT, they have been able to communicate more openly and have been encouraged to participate in decision making.

My research has brought about changes in my behaviour. I have come to understand my role as a leader and that of the SMT in a collegiate approach. As a result of this I have become more confident and comfortable in that role. I have learnt that I need to challenge my assumptions. In some instances my assumptions mitigated against my achieving my aims. I am now more aware of the requirements of effective delegation. I have become more confident in my SMT and now delegate more tasks to them. As a result of my research I have become a more reflective leader, developing teams and encouraging teams and individuals to become thoughtful agents of improvement. I have shown that when staff are involved in discussing issues concerning the school, they develop a common understanding of dilemmas, from which much richer strategies for whole school development can emerge. Because there is real involvement in participation, teachers develop a feeling of belonging, ownership and responsibility for the outcomes.

The Way Forward

When I set out on this enquiry I did not expect to gain so much from the action research. I had expectations that it would solve my concerns, but it has done much more than that. I am now committed to using it in my work. I am also committed to encouraging others to use it. I would like the school to develop into a forward looking, self-reflective research environment and to develop 'enquiring teachers, who are willing to challenge tradition and their own assumptions and to test out and develop new ideas' (Vulliamy and Webb, 1991:234). I would also like to help the SMT identify their training needs and develop their team building and maintenance skills; encourage and support staff to go on management courses; develop a full induction entitlement for all staff; produce an SMT handbook; and continue to identify and provide for my own training and development needs. I believe that action research can help me address some of these aims.

Chapter 3

A collaborative exercise to encourage ownership by staff of the monitoring and evaluation process in a college of further education

Dawn McKen

The White Paper *Education and Training in the Twenty-First Century* (DES, 1991) and the subsequent Further Education Act led to the need for colleges to put in place effective systems to improve their quality and contribute to their own efficiency and effectiveness. My own College responded by creating a quality development unit and in January 1992 I became the new Quality Development Manager. My job was to co-ordinate the existing functions of validation, monitoring and evaluation. I was to work full time within the unit, with administrative support provided by a full-time secretary, an examinations officer, a quality development administrator, part time secretaries, and data input assistants.

Where there is a public commitment to quality, the focus for quality improvement often is associated with the introduction of systematic college-wide monitoring and evaluation systems. When administered in a bureaucratic manner the result can be a paper exercise rather than a real change in practice. For example, in the past the requirements of monitoring consisted of the preparation of basic crude performance indicators for the Local Education Authority. These were not useful for comparison since no criteria had been agreed at either college or county level regarding the meaning of the indicators. Given recent changes to the Further Education sector such as formula funding, delegation and the new requirements of the Further Education Funding Council, colleges are now dependent for funding on indicators of performance. It has become clear that a system capable of providing the necessary statistics in a valid and clear format is vital. I also believe that monitoring and evaluation need to be integrated with other relevant college functions, some of which might be difficult to measure: for example, how student entry to and progression from a programme are prepared for and supported, how motivated the staff are and what morale is like, and how the implications of ethnic diversity, gender and special needs are addressed.

By definition, a performance indicator is a structure, numerical or verbal, for giving information in a form which signals a judgement or provokes a pattern of enquiry. One challenge was to identify and agree a pattern of indicators which would act as a motivating force to improve quality whilst giving a valid measurement of the quality achieved. But this provides only part of the total picture. To be effective the monitoring and evaluation process had also to be a force for change and improvement. I would further distinguish between monitoring as an essentially continuous process and evaluation as an activity which involved the participants in ascribing values and making judgements. In practice it seemed to me so often that a monitoring and evaluation system designed by management was seen as a paper exercise by those charged with its implementation. There was clearly a danger in having a system which appeared impressive on the surface but which was not owned by those most involved. Such a system would be unlikely to encourage critical reflection and active participation by all those involved in the process.

Quality Matters (FEU, 1991) emphasised the belief already made explicit by Pam Lomax (1989b) and others that any approach to quality improvement should be designed or chosen with learners in mind. I took this to mean that the criteria for an appropriate model should

- ❐ primarily seek to improve the quality of teaching and learning;
- ❐ be flexible;
- ❐ harness the commitment of staff;
- ❐ involve the learner in improving the process of teaching and learning;
- ❐ establish the measurement of requirements and of success or otherwise in meeting those requirements, in all functions, in order that progress can be made.

As an FE manager, I reflected that the 1990s looked set to become the decade when everyone who worked for an enterprise would be seen as helping to run the business (Prospect Centre, 1991). The recognised management responsibilities had gradually become devolved – from the senior management in the 1970s, to middle managers in the 1980s, and to all the qualified workforce in the 1990s. According to Peters and Waterman (1982), the key question of any leader is, What have I changed today? and if the answer is Nothing, then the organisation will die. Imposed change is unlikely to enhance the learning process particularly in an educational context. Ideally, educational leadership needs to be seen as a social process, facilitating shared experiences which harness the talents and energies of everyone in the organisation.

There are a number of useful models of leadership that I have drawn upon. For example, Marsh (1989) proposes a model of academic leadership in further education based on the following cyclical process:

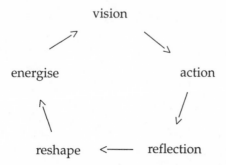

Similarly Handy (1989) links the academic and the management approaches and visualises the wheel of learning as the basis of the driving force of change:

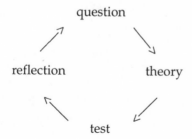

The wheel starts with a question, a problem to be solved, a dilemma to be resolved, a challenge to meet. If it doesn't start there and it is not **our** question, we shall not push the wheel round to the stage of reflection. It won't become part of us.

My aim was to encourage ownership of the monitoring and evaluation process. From the outset I saw the monitoring and evaluation role primarily in terms of developing self-evaluation by course teams. Autocratic leadership, even a successful sell approach, did not seem to me to provide the mechanisms required to empower staff to respond to the changes with which they were faced. It seemed probable that a leadership style based on, and seen to encourage, reflective action would be most likely to further my aims, particularly as my position was one of influence rather than control. I was confident that my intention was not simply a sound idea but had a firm foundation in both managerial and academic theory. However, I had doubts which centred on whether this could be research, particularly in terms of the current climate in the college and the time span for evaluation. I saw that action research could have a pivotal role to play in shifting the culture, but I was also sceptical whether action research would prove to be anything other than good management practice.

My understanding of action research

The distinction between action research and good management practice became clearer to me in my own particular context as I read Richard Winter's (1987) explanation of the forces of collaboration in action research. Here I found tangible evidence of something more than good management practice where action research has the power to add greater depth to the classic cycle of *plan, act, observe and reflect* that I had normally associated with good management practice. Perhaps the words surrounding such a cycle have become too familiar to have any real meaning and there is now a need for a different vocabulary more pertinent to the 1990s, for example *question, listen, think and change*. Within this different vocabulary I see myself as a living contradiction (Whitehead, 1985) where there is conflict between the educational values I hold and the negation of these in my practice. The tension caused by this contradiction moves me to imagine alternative ways of improving my situation.

In her book *Action Research: Principles and Practice*, McNiff (1988) provides a coherent overview of the growth of action research and makes the point that action research is never static but feeds from itself. I used her framework as a starting point in my investigation into the development of action research. I was reassured to discover that two of the essential elements of action research, democratic collaboration and participation, did not arise from educational research but were introduced as a way of focusing on social issues by the American social psychologist Kurt Lewin. I say reassured as his theory established positive links in my mind to both the familiar management cycle and to good practice in the process of monitoring and evaluation.

My understanding also encompasses Lawrence Stenhouse's work of the 1960s and 1970s describing teachers as researchers engaged in 'systematic enquiry made public' (Stenhouse, 1975) and giving credibility to their judgement of their own practice. Following Stenhouse, Stephen Kemmis developed the action research cycle from the work of Kurt Lewin. I must admit that his more structured educational action research model – a diagrammatic example of Lewin's original concept of planning, acting, observing and reflecting – appeared too constricting for my purpose.

However, it was his explanation of 'the four things action research is not' (Kemmis and Henry, 1984) which helped me start distinguishing action research from good management practice. My understanding of the action cycle at that time was completed by reading about the refinements to the self-reflective spiral suggested by Elliott and Ebbutt (McNiff, 1988).

There were two main reasons for my feeling that structured models of action research would be too constricting for my purposes. They cannot deal with novel situations within the main focus and they are not in themselves educational. I felt that close adherence to any particular model could act as a constraint and work against the creative and unknown aspects in action research. I hoped to explore related problems as and when they arose without losing sight of the main focus of my research. Each practitioner, truly to work as an action researcher, builds a framework for research that allows them to interpret the fundamental concepts of action research in an individualistic way. The vital concepts that are at the heart of both the process of action research and its validity are those of reflexive and dialectical critique and collaboration.

Winter (1989) explains in his book *Learning from Experience* that a general theory of dialectics relates the nature of reality and the process of understanding it, revealing its true meaning in the art of discussion. Action research uses dialectics to encourage lateral thinking or, in strategic management terms, to think the unthinkable. Whereas positivism often seeks to ignore the complexity of elements, the dialectical approach investigates the overall context of relations, seeking to expose the structure of internal contradictions beneath the apparent unity. In this connection, MacNeile Dixon (1939) explored the theme of discord in the thinking of Heraclitus, the overall conclusion being that, in looking for truth, you should expect the unexpected.

The impetus to find answers often excludes such processes and has a direct bearing on leadership styles. Management practice normally seeks to solve problems whereas action research encourages problem posing. One of my aims has been to seek to formulate questions rather than to concentrate on being able to give answers. I wish to embrace a dialectical approach where the art of the dialectic is not the art of being able to win every argument. The art of questioning is that of being able to go on asking questions, that is, the art of thinking (Gadamer, 1975).

The action research process

The programme that supports action research at Kingston University is carefully structured so that students are encouraged to write their dissertation as their research progresses rather than after it is finished. At the start students are asked to complete an action research planner along the lines:

What is my concern?
Why am I concerned?
What can I do about it?
How will I know that I have been successful?

This is not as simple as it seems and it takes most students several weeks to clarify the focus of their action research and make their plans. The evolution of the focus for my research is detailed in the development of my proposal and, although naive, it shows my changing role within the college and my growing understanding of action research during the early stages of my enquiry. The changing focus of my concern, numbered from 1-6 below, is listed in chronological order over a period of six weeks culminating in my final focus. Each statement is followed by a summary of my reflection following later directed reading and discussions with support set and tutors at the University and with colleagues at work.

> **1. The ability of programme managers to construct measurable action plans as part of the course review and evaluation process.**

Here my concern is solely about the practice of others; I know the answers and will impose my ideas. The action plan is seen in isolation from the process of monitoring and evaluation and the emphasis is on the writing of the plan rather than on its effectiveness in practice.

> **2. The ability of programme managers to construct action plans as a tool for positive change and improvement.**

My concern is still about the practice of others and I still hold the only key to the answers but some thought has been given to the action purpose of the action plans.

> **3. I want to improve the use of action plans within the course review and evaluation process as a tool for positive change and quality improvement.**

This is the first acknowledgement of the need to shift to personal involvement with the use of 'I want' terminology. I still see the change purely in terms of the practice of others. I remain an observer, solely the change-agent of the actions of my colleagues.

> 4. I am concerned that during the implementation stage of the course review and evaluation policy more time and resources will be spent on the compilation and analysis of statistical performance indicators than on the development of the process as a tool for positive change and quality improvement.

This is the first recognition of personal involvement and concern for my own actions: my acceptance of the contradiction in the purpose of monitoring and evaluation reflects my growing understanding of both my new role and the theory of dialectics related to action research.

> 5. How to gain consensus with colleagues as to the best way to measure the effectiveness and efficiency of student learning programmes so that we can use monitoring and evaluation as a positive vehicle for quality improvement within the context of the new corporate strategy of the college.

I am finally seeing the need for colleagues as collaborators, but still only in the limited terms of gaining consensus rather than as a resource.

> 6. My concern is that my current practice leads me to find answers to problems/changes and to impose my own solutions on colleagues rather than to work with them through a period of uncertainty, exploring alternative avenues and outcomes.

Now my concern is central to my own practice and I realise a change in practice through intervention and reflection might be possible and beneficial. I intend to undertake the research in order to gain further understanding instead of imposing a preconceived idea, and have embraced the need for colleagues as collaborators.

These first weeks of my enquiry were crucial in providing a springboard for the research that followed. The recurring themes of reflection, dialectics and collaboration were brought to the surface and identified as the key issues underlying my proposed action research. The development of the monitoring and evaluation process then became not an end in itself but the vehicle for the development of my leadership skills. At this stage I felt I had almost stumbled on this understanding by chance but in retrospect these feelings were probably tied to my newly-discovered personal involvement. One of the strengths of action research is the intensity of discovery for oneself. Theory and accounts of the experiences of others can provide insight but it is only when that insight is internalised that the true action researcher can emerge. Thus the development of my proposal provided both a reconnaissance stage and, to some extent, the first cycle of my ongoing enquiry.

It is worth considering how and why the evolution of the focus for my enquiry took the course outlined above. Joining the Master's programme had been a last-minute decision. I was perhaps complacent in my attitude towards another research project. The title of my thesis for the DMS programme had been 'Improving Staff Development as a Management Tool'. I had erroneously assumed that it was the result of action research because the research had taken place in my work setting and had involved critical recommendations for improvements.

This superficiality extended to my acceptance of the tutor group as a congenial way to spend time at the college. I found the introductory lecture on Action Research stimulating rather than revolutionary and by the third week I was still confident that I was treading on familiar ground. It all seemed very similar to the way I had always worked. I felt comfortable with the words given emphasis such as planning, evaluating, reflection, collaboration, values, contradiction, et cetera because I saw them only in terms of my past experience, an echo of what Winter (1989) describes as '... the unknowable relationship between external reality and the subjective experience of the person making the judgement'. It was therefore not surprising that, at this stage, I saw completion of the action research planner as a mere formality.

My first proposal was not applauded by my tutor group. Suddenly my preconceptions seemed of little value and I was thrown into a panic. Others in the group seemed to have insights into the mysteries of action research that I could not perceive. However, as I belatedly engaged with the background reading I began to doubt that my emerging comprehension was entirely in sympathy with my fellow students' understanding of the underlying concepts. One of my support set later revealed that she had written in her diary: 'I think DEM might give up'. This view is hardly surprising given my work circumstances at the time, with seemingly constant upheavals involving constantly changing roles and colleagues.

I had been forced to acknowledge that action research required intervention into my own practice. Learning seldom occurs at a constant pace and there are generally moments of insight when one moves forward in leaps and bounds. I have no doubt that the painful processes contained in these early weeks were the main factors contributing to the later success of the research.

The action

My first action in developing the monitoring and evaluation process at my College workplace was to invite colleagues to join two evaluation workshops, one for section leaders and one for programme managers. I made a conscious effort to expunge preconceived ideas and to open out my thinking. I also had to overcome the culture of the college where those attending meetings expected to be given information, rather than to have their opinions sought. My research was already affecting my practice; a creative meeting with unknown outcomes requires different planning to one which is directed. Even simple considerations such as who to invite and the tone of the invitation requires careful consideration in order to gain colleagues' support and make best use of time. Chairs and tables were arranged, relevant publications were on display and coffee was available. I produced agendas for both meetings but emphasised that they were informal and flexible.

I started each meeting by carrying out a nominal group techniques exercise as a way of opening up the debate on monitoring and evaluation. The exercise was successful and I gained valuable insight into the feelings and concerns of colleagues. However, although contradictions did surface, on reflection I realise I was looking for consensus rather than seeking to use collaboration as a resource. My decision to select participants by invitation and to call separate meetings for Section Leaders and Programme Managers was also based on traditional college practice rather than my own thinking. None the less, the outcome of the exercise was useful in that it engendered a suitably reflective perspective stance for the next part of my research.

I had originally intended to collate all suggestions for improving the monitoring and evaluation process from each meeting and to return them to the groups for ranking in perceived importance. In practice we ran out of time. Because I had been seeking consensus, most responses were positive and in line with my own thinking. I therefore decided to return them to the participants in the form of a questionnaire which would also fulfil the need for feedback from the meetings. Questionnaires were also sent to those who had expressed interest in the meetings but had been unable to attend.

In constructing the questionnaire I used the same phrasing as the participants' responses to emphasise the acceptance of their ideas. I listed them in a format which allowed for a logical flow of the monitoring and evaluation process to aid the staff development aspects of the exercise. The inclusion of a comments column fortuitously allowed for the expression of individual points of view. It is interesting that I was beginning to feel sufficiently confident to open up the debate at this stage, if only as written as against face to face communication. As already indicated, action research can be threatening in that we open our own practices to criticism. Our acceptance and encouragement of this criticism is, I believe, a measure of our own development. This theme has certainly informed my own growth during the research. Whilst my diary traced the various stages in this development, it was only later that the implications became fully clear to me. The meetings had also been valuable in introducing me to members of staff with whom I had little previous contact and opened the possibility of setting up cross-college working parties. The feedback questionnaires included an invitation to join a working party together with a timetable to record availability. Meetings were organised to encourage maximum participation with the minimum burden on volunteers.

Ninety-seven per cent of questionnaires were returned to me and I was able to analyse and return them within two weeks. The speedy return of relevant feedback to collaborators was an important feature throughout the research. Again, the perspective I was bringing to the research at the time resulted in most of the 'tick box' responses bringing few surprises and simply reinforcing my ideas. Where this was not the case I was able to invent a rationale to account for these responses (I was still seeking consensus). I was, however, sufficiently impressed with the interest shown by colleagues through their additional comments to record these in the analysis. Through this process I began to consider qualitative as well as quantitative evidence. For example, 75% of the respondents had indicated that the gathering of data would be made easier by a standard mechanism for student feedback but this was qualified by the following comments:

- ❐   formally yes but a great deal gathered informally
- ❐   horses for courses!
- ❐   should leave room for flexibility
- ❐   different requirements for different programmes
- ❐   would prefer feedback relevant to course

Listing the comments also revealed conflicting views in some cases. The question regarding the staff development value of representatives from other programmes working with our programme team elicited the following disparate responses:

- ❐   an excellent idea, a good way to develop staff
- ❐   not sure about the validity of this question
- ❐   would not always be appropriate
- ❐   may be seen as a sensitive/critical area
- ❐   not relevant
- ❐   good idea, maybe time restraint
- ❐   as a last resort

I was beginning to come to terms with opposing views and with an acceptance of an alternative approach to general agreement. It is possible that in traditional research I would have seen the 'tick box' replies as endorsement of my own views without looking beneath the surface at the underlying conflicts. In doing so, the true value of the research would have been lost.

Instead, I now saw the project working parties as an opportunity for participants to share differing opinions and perspectives on the monitoring and evaluation process. I took some time in choosing the members of the working parties within the constraints of their availability. Four groups were formed, each with members from different faculties and levels of responsibility. My original intention had been to monitor and carry out action research with only one of the groups but having attended the initial meetings of the four working parties I saw how interaction and comparison between all groups could hasten my development and increase the scope and validity of the research.

My research therefore moved freely between all groups. I did not attempt to treat each group's development separately and sometimes changed my practice with one group following the outcomes and reflections from meeting with another group. This approach meant that the groups were able to benefit from each other's good practice and I was able either to develop a further change in my practice or to test out a similar approach with different groups.

Informal feedback throughout the research indicated a positive attitude to the participative approach I was fostering but I was also keen to gauge a more formal/objective response from those involved in the working parties. The analysis of the questionnaire used for this exercise revealed a high level of affirmation to all aspects of the operation and outcomes of the working parties.

The three yes/no questions all received 100% positive answers:

- ❑ Would you be willing to join another working party?
- ❑ Would you recommend others to join?
- ❑ Would you recommend other college activities could benefit from this participative approach?

All participants gave the highest ranking possible in answer to the question:

- ❑ How valuable do you believe this participative approach to be for quality improvement?

Evidence of the collaborative nature of the groups was shown by the uniform highly positive response given to the following group of questions:

How fully do you think:

- ❑ you were able to contribute?
- ❑ others contributed?
- ❑ useful discussion took place?
- ❑ ideas generated were followed through?

It was clear that, although I had reservations about my skills as a facilitator and believed my understanding of collaboration as a resource was limited, the members of the working parties had appreciated their opportunity to be involved in the development of the monitoring and evaluation process and had found the exercise worthwhile. The overall activity was more than justified by its outcomes in terms of improved processes and documentation. This was endorsed by feedback from group members. The interim report showed just how much each group had achieved in the short time available and the revised annual reporting form showed the first stage of its development and how we intended to progress in the future. The implementation of a new three-stage monitoring and evaluation process was planned to commence at the start of the next academic year.

Validation

The limitation of action research methodology in the wider context of educational research revolves around the question of validity. It could be argued that traditional research centres on a contrived objectivity in which numbers give a supposed validity, whereas qualitative data projects a subjective element which some find unacceptable. Qualitative data can, however, stand in its own right and it is the interpretation of this information, along with the resulting questioning, that gives it its validity and advantage. The validity of action research resides in the claims to knowledge offered by practitioners in the public arena. Whilst action researchers are not looking for the same outcomes as traditional research and should not be pushed into a defence of their methodology in the latter's terms, they do not necessarily preclude the use of traditional research methods in their own practice.

At Kingston University validation meetings provide the forum for substantiating the claims derived from students' action research and for providing examples of supporting evidence. I had to complete my workplace research within the time constraints of the University course and it was only by following the action research methodology with rigour that I was able to collect sufficient evidence to substantiate my claims during this period. Data was gained through diary records, observational notes, informal feedback, questionnaires, and interviews with colleagues. I kept a comprehensive diary whose intention was to provide a substantive, methodological and analytic account of the events and behaviours relevant to my research. I was following here the advice of Kemmis and Henry (1984) who recommend a personal diary in which to log ' ... our progress and our reflection about two parallel sets of learning: our learning about the practice we are studying (how our practices are developing) and our learning about the process (the practice) of studying them (how our action research is going)'.

When conducting my research I hoped to demonstrate the advantages of the methodology I had chosen and overcome any limitations by being aware of them. The strengths of action research methodology, summarised by Lomax (1986b), of relevance, emancipation, democracy and collaboration appeared to me not only valid as educational values but also valid in terms of universal ethical values deriving from a common sense of natural justice. These elements later underpinned the claims I made for validity as I explained their application to my research. I was initially convinced that the uncertain conditions created by the college reorganisation and the force of external pressures would overwhelm or inhibit my research. However, as my research developed, I found that not only was the research possible in a climate of change but that it had become a positive and powerful change agent in itself.

My own validation meeting had two aims. First, it was seen as an opportunity to test out my claims to have changed my professional practice by presenting my evidence to a sympathetic but critical audience. Second, if properly conducted by all participants, it would give me an enhanced understanding of the research and enable me to develop further. The meeting was attended by my course tutor, five members of the tutor group, my critical friend from college and an independent validator from my research context. The latter was a colleague who had been introduced to my research as a member of one of the working parties. My presentation took the form of an **introduction** explaining the essence of my research, an overview of the **methodology** used, an explanation of the **claims** put forward, supporting **evidence** for each claim, and a **conclusion** matching my research against the four strengths as defined by Lomax (1986a).

1. Introduction

As all those attending the meeting were by now familiar with my research, my introduction concentrated on putting my research into context by giving an overview of its aims. My original concern in terms of outcomes of the research had been the monitoring and evaluation process and I had seen the use of collaboration solely in terms of participation as part of the classic action research methodology. As time progressed I had noted a distinct shift in focus of a management style which was not just collaborative management as normally defined in terms of participation but a style which sought to exploit collaboration as a resource. The monitoring and evaluation process therefore became a vehicle for action research aimed at developing this newly-discovered management approach.

2. Methodology

I used Lewin's action research cycle to outline my methodology, explaining that it was not specific to teaching. I handed out a time plan of my research which indicated the cycles and spirals and also showed their overlapping nature. I summarised and offered documentary evidence for the different techniques I had employed:

- ❑ various nominal group technique exercises;
- ❑ two questionnaires (one to elicit staff perception of monitoring and evaluation and one to explore reactions to the working parties);
- ❑ my detailed diary record;
- ❑ the continual dialogue with my critical friend;
- ❑ observations made of working parties;
- ❑ structured interviews with members of the corporate management team.

3. Claims and 4. Evidence

I suggested that the claims or outcomes of my research reflected its separate but interlinking strands referred to in my introduction. The claims are presented in boxes and the evidence is described below each box.

> **a. The monitoring and evaluation process has been improved and developed more effectively through working with colleagues in an action research framework.**

The evidence put forward shows increased involvement of colleagues. Sixty out of a total of 260 academic staff participated in the research, with length of service not a significant factor. Evidence also shows improvements in documentation. Comparison of the annual summary forms reveals many improved features of presentation and, more importantly, shows application of many aspects of action research to the process of monitoring and evaluation. Encouragement for course teams to participate more fully and on equal terms is given emphasis throughout the revised form and the change of name from 'Annual Course Review and Evaluation Summary' to 'Annual Programme Progress Report' indicates a move towards ownership of the process by programme teams. Basic headings have been replaced in many cases by leading statements to encourage discussion or by questions to stimulate debate amongst course team members. I now have no doubt that had I been working on this task alone I could not have achieved the level of improvement within a similar time span and that the improvements were directly related to the outcomes of the working parties. A three-stage reporting system and the use of a standard student questionnaire with computer analysis were further outcomes of the working parties that awaited implementation within six months.

> **b. I have furthered my understanding of, and am developing a management style which utilises collaboration as a resource.**

The most compelling evidence I can offer for my understanding and use of collaboration as a resource is my own belief in the benefits to be gained by its use. Once again, I must emphasise the distinction between seeing participation as a way of involving staff for their own good as against gaining consensus and using it as a collaborative resource for all those concerned. It is only in its latter form that it becomes more than just another management technique or leadership style. If nurtured, it can become a powerful and compelling change-agent within an organisation. My findings are in line with those of Roberts (1991): 'More importantly they begin to realise that the techniques they might be using are in fact less important than the fact that they are beginning to reflect on whatever aspect of this practice strikes them as important at the particular time'.

> **c. I have increased my understanding of action research through practice.**

One of the recurring issues for me is the distinction between action research and good management practice. Action research is systematic and involves collecting evidence on which to base rigorous reflection. I have no doubt that I have been more rigorous and systematic in conducting my research than I was in my previous practice as a manager. The workshops, working parties, questionnaires and feedback stratagems were prepared and implemented with meticulous care. It is unlikely that any organisation could contain many of such time-consuming activities within its normal operations. Reason and Rowan (1981) maintain that validity in action research depends more on the personal and interpersonal than on the methodological aspects, also noting that '... good research goes back to the subjects with the tentative results and refines them in the light of the subjects' reactions'. It is noticeable that my awareness was heightened and I was constantly and actively exploring questions in my mind throughout the research. Entries in my diary recounted some of the enjoyment in finding echoes of a more youthful questioning self. My critical friend reported that he had been so impressed by the results from the distinct change in my leadership style that he was looking to adapt these into his own practice as Head of School. It is this kind of unsolicited corroboration that enhances my claims to validity. I must further point out that, for the participants involved and for the culture of the college, the working parties provided a major shift from the accepted hierarchical and punishment-centred structure. The responses made on the working-party questionnaires were particularly positive and all respondents stated they would be willing to join further cross-college ventures. One of the turning points in my personal development was when I realised that collaboration benefited all participants – including me! Benefit appears to be not just in terms of outcomes but also in exposing and developing perceptions and ideas that would otherwise lie dormant. I can trace the stages in this development through notes of the sessions, reflective comments in my diary, and preparatory draft documents.

---

d. I can demonstrate that a collaborative approach can be beneficial to the college and have received commitment from management and colleagues to develop the approach together.

The commitment of top management is a prerequisite for the successful implementation of any quality system. I have involved senior management in my research in part to gain their approval of the outcomes. Having voiced her support for the project, the Principal left me to my own devices. We have met at the conclusion to discuss possible future developments arising from the research. The four recently-appointed Deans of Faculty have been kept informed by copies of all documentation. One Dean became sufficiently interested to join one of the working parties; it was rewarding to see him providing valuable input whilst in no way dominating or inhibiting other members.

I later met with all Deans in order to discuss the implications of the proposed revised monitoring evaluation scheme prior to its implementation. I was confident in answering questions regarding the rationale for the changes since so much discussion had already taken place during the working parties. The proposals gained the positive support of the Deans. The improvements to the monitoring and evaluation process are seen as providing a firm foundation for 'bottom up' quality improvement. This tested approach could now also be used to advantage within the support units of the college. Moreover, the use of organised groups has made some inroads into changing the college culture and has shown the potential for further staff involvement. The Principal supports my claims and has made a commitment that planned facilitator training for relevant staff should take place.

The use of collaboration as a resource may well fit the scenario described by Pascale (1990) in which '... disequilibrium might be a better strategy for survival than coherence and order. A central thrust of this thinking is that internal differences can widen the spectrum of an organisation's options by generating new points of view. These, in turn, can promote disequilibrium and under the right conditions self renewal and adaptation occur'.

5. Conclusion

Having substantiated the evidence for each claim I concluded my presentation in the following words, matching the outcomes of my research against the strengths of action research as defined by Pam Lomax (1986b).

Relevance is a word not always applicable to research carried out by those employed in the further education sector. We accept that theory has no real value for students unless it can be demonstrated to have practical application and yet much of our research ends up collecting dust on shelves. By focusing on an intervention in my own practice, the outcomes of my research have already been of benefit to myself, my collaborators, and to the college. There is evidence to show that these benefits are likely to last and act as a spur for further improvement.

Stenhouse wrote that '... the essence of emancipation ... is the autonomy which we recognise when we eschew paternalism and the role of authority and hold ourselves obliged to appeal to judgement' (Stenhouse, 1983). Action research is *emancipatory* in that it allows us to believe in ourselves. It is NOT scientific method applied to teaching. Action research is a systematically evolving, lived process of changing both the researcher and the situation in which she or he acts. The structure of further education has had a debilitating effect on many staff. Lecturers who were originally appointed because of their skills and managerial ability in industry see these attitudes undervalued, becoming hesitant in making simple decisions and hesitant in taking on responsibility. I see action research as an enabling tool that can achieve ownership of practice whilst encouraging personal accountability. The reactions of many participants in the working parties have shown this to be true. One colleague reflected that this was the first time he had been engaged in decision making at the college for twenty years. He went on to produce a paper on learning strategies!

In the past, *democracy* has been something to encourage in students rather than an activity in which lecturers engage. In seeking to explore the ideas and interpretations of others, I endeavoured to use techniques that allowed people to represent their views without being unduly influenced by others (Lomax and McLeman, 1984). In this way the right to participate on equal terms was open to all those involved in the research. The fact that the participants in the working parties represented different levels of responsibility became a vital ingredient since we were able to view and contrast various perspectives of issues as they arose. Indeed many of the issues themselves were brought to the surface because of the conflicting needs of those represented. Because of the success of this venture invitees joining the next group of working parties will be widened to include support and administrative colleagues in the college.

Collaboration in action research is allied to that of democracy in terms of the opportunity afforded to work with and for my colleagues. It is important to me to use all viewpoints as a collaborative resource, not to gain consensus but to look at the differences between them and to focus on the contradictory elements. It was heartening to hear a colleague, acting as an independent validator, state at the validating meeting that she thought I had been 'very brave not to appear to be in control during the working parties'. One of the most important outcomes of my research has been the identification that the greatest potential for further development exists in determining and implementing the processes that create the optimum conditions for this type of collaboration.

Towards the future

The outcomes of my research were more than I had originally hoped for. One of the practical aspects of collaboration is that the numbers involved in making a proposal give it an added power in the eyes of others. This was noticeable in my discussions with the Dean of Faculty. The staff involvement together with evidence of the research undertaken gained the commitment of the Deans in spite of the pressures and problems they were facing at that time. A distinguishing feature of my previous research was that past recommendations looked impressive on paper but I would have to admit, for a number of very good reasons, that I did not implement them. With action research, implementation is in-built into a system where theory and practice can no longer be treated as separate entities.

The required managerial skills are thus changed from the 1980s cognitive skills allied to the systems theory model to those reflected in the ability to manage and relate to people; to get things done; to see the big picture; to think clearly and demonstrate personal maturity. All these skills can be seen to have an affinity with those of the action research practitioner. A breakdown of the competencies clustered within 'the ability to think clearly' would not seem out of place in an action research manual.

I began my research with some scepticism whether my application of action research would prove to be anything other than good management practice. There is no doubt that the two are closely interlinked and that much that is being written about management for the 1990s can be related to action research practice. The gap, and from my experience it is a considerable gap, is that action research demands reflection on one's own practice, whereas management is still seen in terms of doing something to, or for, others. Facilitator and problem-solving skills training arising from the introduction of processes such as Total Quality Management can, and should complement action research, but are not a substitute for it. My aim now is to carry forward the experience gained from this research to total aspects of quality development within the college, using collaboration as a resource – not as a tool!

Chapter 4

Focusing on pupil behaviour to introduce total quality management into a middle school

Jon Stevens

How can we improve the quality of our practice in our school? Quality is an elusive concept particularly for schools in the primary phase. Good primary practice itself is problematic. Thus 'the "good" in "good primary practice" tends to be asserted but seldom demonstrated ... educational justifications for practice may be tacit rather than articulated ... those with power may assume the right to impose their preferred versions of good practice ... the front of consensus has to be maintained at all costs...' (Alexander, 1992:180).

In my school there are competing beliefs and views of the right way to do things. Quality is not the sole prerogative of the school but something to be negotiated with parents, pupils, feeder schools, communities and perhaps commerce. Any consensus view of what quality education once meant has been challenged by recent legislation that has brought about local management, league tables, parental choice and so forth. One task of a headteacher must be to minimise the gap between competing views so that quality becomes a shared concept of a whole community. A re-evaluation of the role of headteacher is required if the head is to be a quality leader and manager (West-Burnham, 1992).

At the time of the research I was the headteacher of an 8 to 12 middle school set in a large dormitory area in the heart of South East England. The school had 375 children on roll divided into 12 mainstream classes with a special needs class in which children with a physical disability spent part of their time. The staffing consisted of headteacher, deputy, twelve full-time teachers, seven part-time teachers, two special needs classroom assistants, two ancillary helpers, three office staff, a caretaker and five midday supervisors. The organisational structure of the school was based on the year group. Each year group of three classes and three teachers had one of its number designated as year leader.

I began my project to fulfil the requirement of an M.A .Dissertation which was to be the outcome of practitioner action research in an area of my choice. I had recently attended a course on TQM and was keen to begin to implement it in the school. Action research seemed appropriate because it provided me with a philosophy that fitted in well with the need to be self-critical and self-reflective and to analyse team work as demanded by the principles and procedures of TQM. Why did I feel it necessary to introduce TQM? I was concerned that the school lacked clear quality thresholds. More specifically I was concerned with my own performance as a leader/manager in three ways. First, how clear was my own value position relating to quality? Second, how successful was I in communicating this to staff? Finally, did I myself demonstrate quality to staff and others through my daily practice? I was also aware that the Senior Management Team (SMT), as a group, had not functioned as effectively as it should. The following concerns had been voiced by various members of the SMT.

❏   Too often we had not met as agreed and scheduled discussions had not taken place.
❏   There were areas where we had not discussed our aims and objectives and where we possibly disagreed.
❏   We needed to work harder at setting agendas and writing minutes and so give ourselves more direction.
❏   We spent too long discussing items without arriving at decisions readily enough.

It may be that the group lacked a sense of what its aims were and that a key area for research would be the clarification of individual and corporate roles and responsibilities.

My general concerns were thrown into much greater focus by my introduction to the ideas of Total Quality Management (Collard, 1989; West-Burnham, 1992; BP Chemicals, 1992). Looking to implement ideas that took root in industry and commerce might appear anti-educational, the beginning of a mechanistic and product-based view of education. However, the growing literature on management in schools, the setting up of the School Management Task Force and the increased funding for management training were all responses to the need to adapt to the sweeping changes of the 1980s. Total Quality Management is an attempt to apply management principles to education and I believe it should be judged on its ability to deliver. As long as the values that underpin education are kept to the forefront, being seen in the day-to-day practice of the school, and provided these values are shared by all the school staff and permeate the institution, then I see no need to be frightened by techniques and strategies that are taken from industry and commerce.

The research

Because TQM is said to take 2-3 years to implement, I decided to work on laying its foundations by focusing on a small number of key aspects of my practice and school organisation.

❑   I would examine my own values and practice and assess whether TQM was an appropriate vehicle for change. Was I living my values in my practice?
❑   I would focus on my role as leader/manager and involve staff and others in helping me form a view of how to meet customer expectations.
❑   I would involve the senior management team so that the project would become a collaborative one, developing the SMT in terms of quality management.
❑   I would involve the whole teaching staff as co-participants to counteract suspicion and resistance to change.
❑   I would also look at the role of other key personnel such as the administrative officer.

My own role would be crucial both in introducing the idea and principles of TQM and also in developing the SMT in terms of those principles. I was ready to re-appraise my role and that of my senior colleagues, refocusing our job profiles to reflect changing responsibilities and workload. In the light of my concerns I realised that the process by which we agreed outcomes, working plans, areas of concern, priority lists or areas of disagreement, was as important as the outcomes themselves. I saw this as a move towards the 'collaborative cultures' of action research.

I saw my values as a leader implicit within my view of my role which was to:

❑   create and sustain the school's vision;
❑   help individuals to achieve personal and institutional goals;
❑   provide resources to ensure that targets could be met;
❑   ensure that individuals had the knowledge and skills to work effectively;
❑   provide guidance and advice on standards and levels of performance;
❑   give recognition, reward and feedback.

I saw these values as being congruent with the philosophy of TQM and based on the following principles:

❐   involvement of everyone throughout the organisation
❐   striving to achieve the highest possible quality
❐   becoming customer focused
❐   a 'right first time' culture
❐   continual monitoring to improve effectiveness
❐   using data and fact to underpin management
❐   use of structured problem solving methods
❐   commitment to continuous improvement
❐   recognition of good-performance

My vision was about shared responsibility and delegation of meaningful and worthwhile tasks, encouraging personal initiative and seeing people as an asset to be developed. One could ask, 'What has this got to do with the children in the school?' In reply I would suggest that the ultimate test of quality in my school would be the quality of the learning experience that the children received and the progress made. This comes down to classroom practice. The curriculum doesn't exist until a transaction occurs between the teacher and the child. The task of management is to ensure that the school's organisation is best suited to support the teacher in that 'educational transaction', and quality in management will help achieve quality where it really matters, in the classroom.

Researching with the Senior Management Team

I decided to begin the research with an examination of the role of the SMT as I believed that the process of improvement of the functioning of this important team was crucial. I decided to tape the SMT meetings and analyse and validate this data with the assistance of my critical friend (my deputy), the support set of headteachers at the University, and the SMT and staff group functioning as a collaborative and critical community. Their participation would ensure that the research was more than an indulgent exercise in self-reflection. I would also keep a research diary which would document the progress of the research. I intended to focus on the SMT at a number of levels:

❐   to look at how we define quality in a meaningful way;
❐   to look at how the meetings function to achieve a 'quality' result;
❐   to focus on the group's working practices and effectiveness;
❐   to review the role of SMT in the school to ensure that it is, and is seen as, an effective group;

❐   to examine the way the group implements its managerial functions by looking at the responsibilities of its members;

❐   to focus on my role in facilitating this reflective review.

As I wanted to have a clear starting point, we each completed a team analysis sheet which attempted to indicate areas of strengths and weaknesses. Having established the base line of how we saw ourselves as a functioning group, I wanted us to move on to addressing the issues that arose. It was agreed that we would regularly look at how we functioned and that we would tape and discuss a number of our meetings. This I started to do as well as making notes in my research diary of my own reflections and those of my critical friend. By the end of the first three month period I was already identifying areas of concern in the way that the SMT meetings were functioning, and an analysis of the tapes of our meetings led to some general points emerging:

❐   members had their own personal agendas
❐   there were difficulties in keeping to the subject
❐   there were personal animosities
❐   members were unclear as to their roles
❐   there were basic problems with communication
❐   there was no clear consensus on our aims and perhaps our values
❐   the hierarchy was unclear
❐   my role as chairperson was problematic

My emphasis on this work with the SMT was interrupted by two separate conversations that combined to alter the way I saw my project. The first conversation occurred as a result of presenting my interim report at the College at the end of January to my tutor and support set. Their comments were revealing. It was said that my language at times seemed one of control and that I was doing things to people, seeing them as objects. Other questions were asked. Why did my SMT group include only two of the five 'B' post holders in the school? Why, in a school of my size, had I worked with the SMT rather than the whole school? Did this contradict the principles of TQM I was trying to introduce?

The second conversation was one in which I shared the feedback from the Kingston group with the SMT. They immediately picked up the point made about working with the whole staff and suggested we should go to the staff and get them to identify a concrete concern as a focus for applying TQM principles. I was taken aback by this response, which was not part of my plan, but it widened the scope of the research and it had senior management commitment. In terms of the methodology and philosophy of action research and the principles of total quality, the new plan had much to commend it even though it meant me changing direction.

My initial work with the Senior Management Team was useful and interesting although after the decision to take the project to the whole staff was made, it become a side spiral to the main focus of the research (McNiff, 1988). I had started my research at the wrong end of the authority and status pyramid. Murgatroyd and Morgan (1993) see customers at the top of an inverted pyramid, teachers in the middle, and the headteacher at the bottom. In their model the teachers are best able to judge the customers' needs and deliver quality improvement because they are closest to the customers. Management's job is to support the teachers. The whole perspective of my enquiry was undergoing a radical shift. I reflected that earlier, when I had first talked to senior staff about the notion of TQM, their comments, facial expressions and tone of voice spoke volumes about their scepticism. It should have been clear from what they said and how they said it that they regarded this as yet another idea born in theory but rarely lived out in practice. Though the SMT had agreed to participate in the project, one of them had said, 'It sounds like we're making a car, not educating children.' Now, I felt, I had the commitment of the others to the possibility of making a real change in our practice.

However, this early part of the work eventually had one important outcome. At the end of the year the SMT agreed to go back to a larger management team comprising all the 'B' holders in the school plus head and deputy, feeling this would involve all the key members of the teaching staff as well as providing clearer lines of communication back to staff. From a TQM point of view this was sensible and meant that a layer of management had been removed, giving a flatter and more dynamic structure. I do not think this would have happened if we had not had the earlier discussion in the SMT.

Working with the whole staff

As a result of my conversation with the SMT I agreed to call a staff meeting and involve all staff in choosing a practical issue that could be used for the focus of whole school improvement. In this meeting I used a form of nominal group technique (Lomax and McLeman, 1984) so as to ensure that all staff had a voice, not just the more vocal ones. I began by asking them to work individually to identify three issues of concern that they felt we could tackle in the next few months as a school. Dividing into three groups, teachers were asked to discuss their choices and agree and prioritise three areas of concern. All three groups put pupils' poor behaviour and attitudes as their top priority. This was an issue we had indeed looked at and failed to resolve on a number of occasions. It made me question my own attitude to this in the past, which had been to dismiss it as a matter of applying the procedures that already existed better. Had I allowed sufficient discussion? Had I listened to my staff?

The second part of the meeting involved looking at the identified problems and attempting to diagnose where the causes lay. I had previously prepared some 'cause and effect diagrams' for staff to work on. Also known as Fishbone or Ishikawe diagrams, the headings are designed to allow as full an exploration of the problem as possible. This is a brainstorming activity for a group, with the emphasis being on generating all the possible causes, without making any comment on validity or relevance. When they had finished I collected the ideas of each group and wrote them on a large white board. The session ended at that point.

The second meeting of the whole staff, one week later, started with a quick reminder of what staff had put on the cause and effect diagram and from there moved to a consideration of two issues:

❏   What is the good and bad behaviour we want to achieve or avoid?
❏   Who is good behaviour for and why do we want to achieve it?

In groups, I asked staff to identify the stakeholders who would have a legitimate interest in pupils' behaviour. They came up with the obvious groups – parents, children, teachers, other staff, governors, the local and wider community, and visitors to the school. Concern was expressed about parents who might misinterpret our interest in poor behaviour as an indication that it was widespread.

Staff were also asked to consider the aims of the school, looking at each in turn and deciding whether poor behaviour and poor attitudes amongst the pupils would undermine the achievement of that aim. I wanted to raise staff awareness of the general importance of the issue in its wider sense, both to us in achieving our aims, but also to others who had an interest in seeing the school perform in a quality way. At the end of the session I asked the staff to indicate individually on a pro forma what behaviours they deemed acceptable or unacceptable and to relate this to behaviour in different parts of the school as well as in general. This would give us a practical idea of what we really wanted to achieve.

A whole school project

During the staff session someone suggested we should focus on 'Respect' as a theme. Everyone agreed that they would focus on this theme in the classroom, and I said I would take the lead in assemblies. Subsequently I focused my assemblies on a number of aspects that I knew concerned staff:

❏   the tone of voice of children in various situations
❏   using a proper form of address
❏   interrupting staff when talking
❏   opening doors for others, saying 'please' and 'thank you'

- ❑   treating others with respect
- ❑   how do you like to be treated?
- ❑   examples of good and poor behaviour
- ❑   who should you respect?
- ❑   how do you show respect for someone?
- ❑   how have some children shown disrespect?
- ❑   what rights do we all have?
- ❑   bullying

My main aim was to raise pupils' awareness of the issue of behaviour as one that was of concern to the whole school. I did this by making 'Respect' a big issue for children to think about and for staff to reinforce. As the work gathered momentum through the Spring and Summer terms, my colleagues' comments were encouraging as they fed back anecdotal information on improvements they had noticed among the children.

Evaluation

Working with the teaching staff on the issue of behaviour was revealing in a number of ways. The decision to use a more structured approach to solving problems and generating solutions was born out of a concern to apply the principles to TQM. Towards the end of the project I asked staff to complete an evaluation questionnaire about the work. The staff's response indicated that it had led to satisfaction in terms of the outcome and the process. The evaluation broadly indicated that staff approved of a process whereby they had a chance to discuss an issue in small groups and influence the outcome in a clear way. For example, the following written comments were made:

> *I liked having more opportunity to say what I wanted. Sometimes a few of the staff have such strong views it's hard to say anything different. It's also difficult to speak out in front of the staff meeting of over 15 people.*

> *It was a different atmosphere in the discussion group. We all felt more relaxed and it was easier to say what you wanted.*

Winter (1989:43) suggests applying a 'reflexive critique' to accounts so that particular assumptions and judgements are questioned. Using the comments above to question my own practice, I must ask, what lies behind these statements? They clearly mean that I should look at how I elicit staff opinion. How are staff best able to put forward their honest and sincerely felt views? What are their theories of what constitutes a professional discussion? What do they mean by 'strong views' or 'a relaxed atmosphere' and how do these comments highlight their own professional needs? The comments challenged my assumptions about how I run the school and in particular how I run staff meetings. Indeed, the very statement 'how I run' is perhaps indicative of assumptions that are implicit in my view of staff meetings.

I also asked the staff what they thought they had done to make a difference in children's behaviour. Four comments are indicative of the range of views:

I am more vigilant when on duty and walking around the building during the day.

Awareness of behaviour in general has been heightened and consequently I have focused on examples of good behaviour within my class to set a role model for the others.

The whole discussion on behaviour has helped me to sharpen my attitude to behaviour and be more alert to any breaking of the rules.

I feel clearer in what we as staff are expected to focus on and more confident that we are all giving the same message.

The work with the teaching staff had been revealing in terms of their commitment to tackling a practical issue in a 'quality' way – work that would lead to a quality outcome but would also be a vehicle for exploring quality processes. Staff were able to list improvements that they had noticed in the children's behaviour, as well as detail the way they had changed their own approach to the issue. They recognised that better behaviour was the outcome of greater consistency from the staff and children being clearer about what was expected of them. Their comments I believe implied a change in their knowledge and understanding. When staff were asked, what do we need to do next to create a more positive attitude in the children and better management of pupil behaviour? they were able to respond with clear suggestions that have given us direction that will lead to the writing of a school policy on the management of pupil behaviour. It is important that the research has such a public outcome that is of educational significance.

Working with the non-teaching staff

The involvement of the non-teaching staff had also been identified on our initial cause and effect diagram. One of the tenets of TQM is that those closest to the action are often the best at identifying problems and their causes as well as generating solutions. Who after all is closest to the problems that might occur at lunchtime if not the midday supervisors and the catering staff?

Involving the non-teaching staff in the enquiry made me stop and think: How do they regard me in terms of approachability? Do they see me as authoritarian? If there were comments that non-teaching staff wanted to make that might be considered critical, how prepared would they be to make them to me? I was conscious that I had not consulted enough with non-teaching staff.

I persuaded my school administrative officer to lead a session for non-teaching staff. The meeting was timed for immediately after lunch when nearly all would be available. Midday supervisors were paid for an extra session to enable them to stay. I gave each a sheet outlining the principles of TQM and also a copy of the teachers' cause and effect diagram as background information. Nine staff, including midday supervisors, kitchen staff, office staff, special needs classroom assistants and classroom assistants took part. They were asked to produce lists of the problems that they saw in terms of pupils' behaviour and to prioritise them. They were asked to produce suggestions of what they would like to see changed and improved. They were asked what they wanted from teaching staff, senior staff and the headteacher in terms of support and also they were asked what they felt they could do individually and collectively to improve behaviour and attitudes amongst the children.

Data from their meeting came in three ways: a flip chart of their specific agreed suggestions, notes on the meeting made by the Admin Officer, and a recorded interview I had with her shortly afterwards. It is a shame the group did not want to be tape recorded and my information came mainly from my interview with the admin officer.

The list of agreed items detailed below tied in closely with comments made by staff.

Their list of four main problems was as follows:

- ❏ the lack of respect of children to staff and other children
- ❏ the rules were unclear
- ❏ the role of non-teaching staff in enforcing rules was unclear
- ❏ the children's attitudes were poor

A further four problems identified were:

- ❏ noise, particularly in the dining hall
- ❏ the children's inability to queue
- ❏ children misbehaving when carrying tables and chairs
- ❏ spitting

Their list of solutions was as follows:

❏ explain to the children why we have rules;
❏ rules must be issued so non-teaching staff know what we are to expect from children;
❏ there needs to be more liaison between staff and non-teaching staff;
❏ children must be told to respect both adults and themselves.

Involving the non-teaching staff was important because it was a way of involving them more closely in the work of the school. Most tellingly, I learned that they sometimes felt isolated from the school. They felt that they were not given enough opportunity to be involved in the praising and encouraging side of helping pupils achieve good behaviour. Their role was too often one of admonishing children. This was especially true of the midday supervisors. Non-teaching staff wanted to be more involved in the school's activities and to feel 'part of a team'. The following points were summarised by the admin officer and reported back to me:

❏ We do not have a natural authoritative role and so we require well-defined rules and regulations as guidelines which must be pointed out to children also.
❏ We require support from senior staff when rules are not followed.
❏ We do want to feel more involved with the life of the school and have a role, perhaps being a member of a school house, by being involved in sports days.
❏ We want to know what is going on in the school and to have more information on what is happening.
❏ We would like to give praise rather than just scold for bad behaviour. Could we give house points for good behaviour or good manners or helping out?

It is unfortunate that I do not have the participants' own words to reflect these concerns more accurately. I have to wonder whether the Admin Officer has reflected the non-teaching staff's concerns accurately. Does the list of concerns reflect more her own views? The information as it stands is incomplete and unreliable, yet there is a need for the non-teaching staff to be involved further, because it is one of their strong demands that they have a clearer role and are more involved. The writing of a school policy on the 'Management of Pupil Behaviour' with their involvement and views taken account of, would clearly provide part of the response they require.

However, the non-teachers do not see the problem in terms of themselves. All their concerns and areas for change lie outside themselves. What could they do themselves to bring about improvement? How far do problems that they have described reside in their own deficiencies or mistakes? A fuller understanding of the problem is still needed and I am hesitant to draw conclusions from such limited information. What is of greater interest to my study and how it relates to quality is the fact that here we have a large group of staff who seem to be left out of the decision making structure and clearly feel it. In a TQM institution one of the first questions ought to be, 'What can I do to tackle this problem and make an improvement to quality?' A change in attitude to that is a long way off and I am not at all surprised by the 3-5 year span that is given to achieving Total Quality principles in an institution.

Working with the children

After discussion with the staff, I decided to ascertain children's views on their own behaviour and what they felt about the recent emphasis on 'respect'. We devised a questionnaire to give to every child in the school. The staff played a major role in getting feedback from the children in their classes. It was clear from the returns that different staff had placed differing degrees of importance and value on this. Some teachers had clearly spent a good deal of time talking through the questions with the children and giving them sufficient time to give clear and if necessary detailed answers. Other questionnaires by contrast were incomplete with sloppy answers, suggesting that teachers had not spent time briefing the children. Clearly the results of the questionnaire have been devalued as a result and this is disappointing to me. I realise now that we should have tried out the questionnaire with one or two classes ensuring that the process was well documented. We should also have spent more time considering how the questionnaire was administered.

I think it is important that the children were asked their opinions and some of the results have been fed back at assemblies. I am sure we do not ask children their opinions and views often enough. Though the survey had weaknesses, some of the results were illuminating. In particular there were three areas that have brought out interesting information.

Praise and encouragement

A positive view of their achievements and good self esteem is an important prerequisite of good behaviour across the school so it is important that children appreciate the system of positive feedback we operate. 'Special mention in assembly' and 'the certificate of achievement' that goes with it were popular ways of rewarding good behaviour across all ages, but the children's responses challenged the way we used other rewards in the school. In particular their assessment of house points was different to the importance we give to them in the school and has caused us to question their worth. House points elicited a definite division in response with the lower two years preferring house points to the older ones. This clear division might reflect differences in the way teachers respond to this way of praising and encouraging children. We might ask, How are house points awarded? Are they announced in front of the class or are they awarded in a quiet way? We must decide what elements to include and how consistent to be in their application.

Bullying

51% of all the children who responded to the question, 'What behaviour upsets you in school that you really don't like to see?' mentioned bullying. This came as a great surprise to me and my colleagues. We have always considered our school to have a very low incidence of bullying and that which has occurred has seemed to be of a minor kind. Do we have a much higher incidence of bullying than any of us realised or are children perhaps very aware of and sensitive to the little bullying that goes on? Bullying was highlighted in the assemblies about respect. Have the children responded by reflecting this back, a concern that the staff and I have helped to create? Whatever the source of children's perceptions, this was very worrying to me and is something I intend to follow up in the new term with a particular focus on bullying as part of our wider strategy of improving children's attitudes and behaviour.

Unfair treatment

Of even greater significance was that 52% of children in Years 6 and 7 commented on the way they were treated in school as being unfair. This is a figure that cannot be ignored even though it cannot just be taken at face value. Does it illustrate that the children have good memories of a few incidents of unfairness, or are the staff unheedful of the need for scrupulous fairness in their dealings with children? This brought home the point to all the staff that we have to work hard at being fair, and being seen to be fair. A sizeable number, especially in the top two years, remarked that they did not like to see whole class punishments and felt their views were not taken into account.

> *When the boys are being silly some of the girls are as well and when an adult finds out about it they just blame the boys.*

> *When delivering punishments, teachers should attempt to gain a full picture of what happened from witnesses etc.*

> *Teachers having pets ... if they misbehave the teacher sometimes turns a blind eye.*

These views require us as sensitive teachers to ask whether we should talk to the children more and also whether we can say that we are fair, honest and reasonable in our dealings with the children. I could have involved the children in a more direct and interactive way by talking about these behaviour issues with classes yielding more direct information. This is something I intend to pursue.

Reflections on the project

I feel that the information I have gathered has led me to a deeper understanding of the problems though not necessarily to achieving a solution to my initial concern, that is, how does one define and achieve quality across the whole school? It is certainly true that the work has raised more questions than it has answered. This however is a strength of the action research method rather than a weakness. It is indeed the raising of questions that leads to reflection and the development of one's understanding of one's professional context and practice (Kemmis and Henry, 1984:8).

Whitehead (1989) asks questions with which one can judge the validity of one's claims to knowledge:

(a) Was the enquiry carried out in a systematic way?
(b) Are the values used to distinguish the claim to knowledge as educational knowledge clearly shown and justified?
(c) Does the claim contain evidence of a critical accommodation of propositional contributions from the traditional disciplines of education?
(d) Are the assertions made in the claim clearly justified?
(e) Is there evidence of an enquiring and critical approach to an educational problem?

Such questions as these need to be explored and discussed throughout the time of the research to ensure that it is disciplined, systematic, rigorous, relevant and valid. Co-researchers and critical friends are essential if the work is to have worth. Meaning is constantly re-negotiated through discussion and interaction in our daily lives. The 'observe, reflect, plan, act' cycle should be a collaborative attempt to change what we do and what we know. Our claims to know require the view of the other.

What claims emerge from the results of the research presented here? They are more general than I would have wished. My substantive findings are limited and I feel that much of what I have done is to establish more clearly the context in which I am working. The questions being asked are now clearer and more deeply focused. My claims are as follows:

1. As a staff we have worked on the issue of behaviour together and through applied strategies we have begun to put in place a framework for collaboration to improve what we do in a structured way, a way that allows for maximum involvement and ownership.

2. We have laid the groundwork to enable us as a school to draw up a 'Management of Pupil Behaviour' policy with much clearer aims, and a better understanding of the practices and procedures that are most likely to lead to quality in terms of desired pupil behaviour.

3. My investigation has made me question my practice. It has made me look more closely at how I involve staff in a truly democratic and empowering way.

4. I have a deeper understanding that the achievement of quality lies not only in having clear values and aims, but also in ensuring that these are shared by other staff and that there are clear and agreed procedures and practices that lead towards the achievement of quality.

5. My own understanding of my position in the school has deepened and I appreciate far more the importance of my role supporting staff in achieving quality.

6. I have raised many questions in the course of my research which have caused me to reflect on my practice and deepen my professional understanding and knowledge.

My view of my role as enabler has been enhanced by my understanding of Total Quality Management and by my early and flawed attempts to explore its introduction. I believe so much more strongly in the importance of placing staff's perceptions and views at the heart of decision making. The idea of the inverted pyramid very much appeals to me as a sensible model for a school. It is important constantly to remind oneself of the primary function of the institution and who delivers that function. The teachers and support staff are ultimately the deliverers of quality education, and one of my main jobs has to be assisting them to do that to the best of their ability. I am not saying that this inverted pyramid takes away from the headteacher, his or her task of leadership. What it does do is to change the perspective of that leadership which sees the managerial function as a service to internal customers, and the needs of those internal customers (teachers primarily) have to be met. This challenges me to ask a number of questions of myself. What is it that I do to support the real deliverers of quality in the school and how do I know that I do it successfully and to the satisfaction of the staff? Do I know what it is that the staff want from me in terms of support? Have I ever asked them what quality service from me would look like? These are challenging questions that have serious implications for my management of the school, and which I wish to pursue in the future.

One interesting and unforeseen outcome in terms of my own understanding was the realisation of the links between action research and TQM. This is perhaps a surprising notion given their different starting points. Action research has its origins in a radical research tradition while TQM comes from a managerial/capitalistic perspective. Despite their different parenthood and their different purposes there are some striking similarities:

1. Both TQM and action research operate as both methodology and philosophy, with general principles to be followed to achieve the desired result.

2. Both methods start from a statement of beliefs. In action research these beliefs are values that are not being lived out in practice. The values underpin the practice and are the starting point for the need for action. In TQM the key belief or value is held by all and is stated in terms of a mission or vision statement. The vision acts as a guiding force to which the school is working.

3. Democracy and empowerment are powerful elements in both ideologies. Action research is about researchers setting their own research programmes based on their own concerns that they have isolated in their educational practice; they work with colleagues and not upon colleagues. For quality to be achieved with TQM real power and decisions belong to the individuals and teams who actually deliver quality to their customers.

4. Both traditions have an imperative to change and see continuous improvement as part of the nature of the good researcher or the quality institution.

5. Both rely on data and evidence to indicate exactly what the problem is and to make judgements about the best possible solutions. Data collection methods are different but in both cases data is to be used in a public way.

6. Both methodologies emphasise process. Quality resides in action and not simply in defining it or trying to say what it looks like.

This enquiry convinced me of the applicability of TQM to schools. Whilst its obvious application in education would seem to be to the secondary and FE sectors, I am sure it can be adapted to primary schools. In many respects it should be easier where processes are generally simpler and teams are less complicated. The implementation of the National Curriculum, the debate about assessment and its reporting, the discussion of a value added element – these changes have made primary schools more sensitive to the need to have some measure of the quality of their work. The beginning of OFSTED inspections in 1994 in the primary sector has surely hastened that process.

I have said on a number of occasions that this work has raised many questions for me. In some respects I feel that I have more than I started with. However I am conscious that I have gained many insights that I did not have before. Of greater importance is that I now have a much deeper understanding of how I can manage my school with the greater involvement and, I hope, satisfaction of all the staff.

Chapter 5

Enhancing the image of a first school in the immediate and wider community

John Loftus

How can we enhance the image of our school to meet the demands of an ever competitive situation in such a way that we remain true to our values for the education of young children? As an acting headteacher of a multi-ethnic first school in an outer London Borough I worked over the period from July 1991 to January 1992 to execute an action research project of which this was my main aim. I became acting head because the head had taken early retirement and the deputy was due to start maternity leave; the post was advertised for one term only until the school could set in motion procedures for appointing a new head.

The reason that I decided to concentrate on marketing was that we were an infant school in a situation of falling rolls and I was concerned that as eight-year-old children transferred to other schools, some of them primary schools, parents would take their younger siblings with them. We were also hidden away from the main road and bus routes so we did not get noticed by passing traffic.

Originally, I did not envisage myself as 'marketing' my school. I was aiming to 'enhance its image'. Through my reading however, I learnt that 'marketing is practised to some degree in every school in the country, although it may be called something else – school community relations, public information, or communications with parents' (Hardie, 1991:17) and 'any activity identified with the school is marketing an image of the school'

(Fletcher, 1991:13). At the beginning I subscribed to the view that marketing was not an activity associated with education and like many other teachers considered it to be unprofessional. The idea that schools were in competition with each other, were *selling* their curriculum, seemed unethical. Yet, a justification for marketing schools can be found in the two major Education Acts of 1980 and 1988. The 1980 Education Act created the conditions in which marketing became important by encouraging competition between schools and by signalling to parents that they were the new 'customers' and 'clients' (Stott and Parr, 1991:1). Sections 6 and 7 of the 1980 Act reduced the circumstances in which admission to a school may be refused; section 3, by allowing parents to send children of compulsory school age across LEA boundaries encouraged competition between neighbouring LEAs; sections 17 and 18 increased competition between the public and private sectors with the introduction of the 'Assisted Places Scheme'; and section 8 obliged LEAs to describe their policies and processes in a directed form so that parents could have greater insight into what the schools had on offer (Brunt, 1989). The 1988 Reform Act moved the marketing of schools even further. Given demand, schools were obliged to admit as many pupils as the school building would actually hold. With formula funding, resources were linked to the size of pupil roll. Both the abolition of catchment areas and the policy of open enrolment meant that primary school headteachers and their staff needed to think very carefully about their relationship with parents and the local community (Hardie, 1991:7). The national curriculum became the 'product on offer' (Harrison and Gill, 1992:117) and parents could compare its provision in different schools by looking at SATS results, which were intended to provide a national yardstick against which the performance of schools could be measured. A final factor that has pushed primary schools into the competitive arena has been the falling demand for school places brought about by demographic change.

Although the incentive to undertake this action research project can be seen in the conditions brought about by educational legislation, my own educational intentions played the major part in determining the view I came to take of marketing and the way in which I set about implementing a marketing policy. My early reflections led me to the following insights:

❒ that when a school is proud of the education it offers, then the community, both immediate and wider, should be made aware of this, and that any marketing which a school carries out should have the aim, as an end result, of improving the resourcing for the children of that school;

❒ that marketing of a school should benefit both the school, immediate community, and wider community (e.g. industry) alike, and that a broader curriculum for our children creating greater learning opportunities (e.g. 'hands on' experience of the world of industry) would result because of this;

❏ that all staff (teaching and ancillary) should be encouraged to feel a joint commitment for the marketing of their school, and that marketing should be viewed as existing solely for the children of the school and not be perceived as a means to an end.

I hoped to create the situation whereby the teaching staff, welfare staff, nursery nurses, caretaker, secretary, governors, children and parents were involved in promoting our school. I wanted to make the school curriculum more accessible to parents and the school aims transparent to the broader community. I wanted to involve our children and their work in creating an educational image for the school.

Action research and marketing

It was because of these educational intentions that I chose to use action research as the methodology for my project. I was influenced by the Kingston University model of action research (Lomax, 1994b, 1995a) which is fairly eclectic but is premised on a number of principles:

❏ that its aim is educational improvement;
❏ that it incorporates the self-development of the main researcher and the other people that become involved;
❏ that it is rigorous and self-critical of assumptions; and
❏ that its outcomes are made public.

The collaborative intent of these principles was particularly important as I intended to work with staff, governors, the inspectorate, parents and pupils. All these parties would have different perceptions of our school which I could use to promote its image and thus 'go public'.

I was also influenced by McNiff's model of action research which describes a main spiral of activities from which there would be a number of side-spirals (McNiff, 1988:44) because this seemed to be a good way of representing what I anticipated to be a number of problem-solving manoeuvres. I was coming to a new school not knowing any of the governors, staff, parents, children; not knowing any of the policies or practices which were common to that particular school. All this, plus the new initiatives with which I would have to deal, such as implementing the new History and Geography National Curriculum, dealing with compulsory competitive tendering and introducing staff appraisal, to name but a few. I saw that McNiff's model would allow for the 'spontaneity' and 'flexibility' I would require to complete the project in the time available before a new headteacher was appointed. Figures 5a and 5c are representations of my research up to this point. They use a version of the McNiff spiral and may be seen to support the view of Lomax and Parker

(1995) that action researchers should be working towards ways of representing their work that are unique to their own particular meanings and contexts.

As I was to present the outcome of this project as a dissertation for an MA, I knew that I would have to provide evidence for the claims I would make and therefore I set up the mechanisms for monitoring the project carefully. I used a learning log/diary to record meetings, discussions, observations and events throughout the duration of my project. Questionnaires were given to every parent. SWOT (strengths, weaknesses, opportunities, threats) pro formas were completed by all the governors and the teaching and ancillary staff. Important meetings were minuted. Children's perceptions of the school and of the things they liked about it and how it could be improved were recorded on audio tape. I also used photography to record 'before' and 'after' improvements to the physical image of the school. All this work was reinforced by reading the relevant literature, and its interpretation was made subject to on-going discussion with a support set of MA students and a critical friend. My critical friend was a governor at the school who I met at the first governors' meeting that I attended as acting head. During a discussion of formula funding, she said that we needed to find ways of marketing the school: 'I find this marketing in school fascinating; it's something I'd like to know more about' (from my notes of meeting). My response was to invite her to collaborate with me on the action research.

Spiral 1
Projecting an image of the school to parents

At the start of my action research I had numerous conversations with key individuals, drawing on their experience and particular expertise to enhance my own understanding of the situation and to inform my choice of action. An early meeting with my chair of governors and another parent governor resulted in a practice that I have continued, a morning 'walk about' the school, to be seen personally to welcome the parents and children. By doing this I got to know the parents and children extremely quickly. Parents began to stop and talk to me about aspects and worries of school life and I was able to reflect on these and incorporate them into my action plans. I found that ten minutes in the morning was not enough time to deal with all issues and therefore I introduced the idea of a 'surgery' which I held every Tuesday afternoon. This surgery ran for the duration of my project and up to my leaving the school.

I quickly learned that parents were not at all clear about the aims and intentions of the school and that much of the current language used to explain their children's education was unintelligible to them. This was particularly problematic for the ethnic minority parents, many of whom felt excluded because of their different language background. I imagined the solution to the problem as having three dimensions:

- the first was a short term solution which I was able to put into immediate action;
- the second was a medium term solution which involved working with staff and pupils; and
- the third was a longer term solution, trying to involve parents who did not necessarily come into the school.

The short term solution was one upon which I could act quickly. A discussion with my link inspector spurred me to devise an information display for parents, to explain key educational concepts that were usually referred to by abbreviations. This involved first visiting a school that had introduced this idea, then producing a similar display which I put in the main entrance foyer next to the parents' area, where it would gain maximum exposure. At the same time I tried to make our ethnic minority parents more welcome by displaying a welcome poster in 35 different languages in the main entrance facing the doorway for all to see.

I then began a series of meetings with staff to discuss the importance of providing the 'right' image to parents and to devise strategies for achieving this. We began by considering the needs of our ethnic minority pupils and parents and identified the importance of making sure that the curriculum reflected their cultures. Two policies were drawn up: an anti-racist policy and a resourcing policy to support a multicultural curriculum. The anti-racist policy stressed the importance of working with the children to reduce racist attitudes. The Borough co-ordinator for multicultural music and dance was contacted and she was able to arrange for a group of school girls to visit the school for an afternoon of Asian dance, singing and musical instruments. Our children then wrote illustrated 'thank you' letters, and a display of these was mounted in the high school. This episode had a dual outcome: it met the needs of my school's ethnic minority parents and pupils; but my school was also receiving coverage and publicity in a high school. This provided the incentive for spin-off spiral 1a, developing a more multicultural curriculum, which does not form part of this account and spin-off spiral 1b, involving the pupils in developing and marketing a pupil-centred image of the school, which became central to the whole project and is discussed in more detail later.

My medium term solution was to work with the teachers to compile a letter to parents to explain what was happening in the school regarding the curriculum. The letter described attainment targets through a topic and explained how parents could assist in the delivery of the topic and how they could help in the classroom generally. Each class teacher handwrote and photocopied the letter for the parents of the children in their respective classes in order to make the communication as personal as possible. This led to my longer term solution. Working with staff on devising a simple questionnaire for parents and analysing their responses, we aimed to establish whether the school was meeting their needs. The results of the questionnaire were discussed by the staff and the governors. We considered: Do people feel welcome when they come into the school? Can they find the school office, library, welfare room, etc? Do they get enough information? Do they feel their children's academic needs are met? Are they happy with the reputation of the school? Can they contact governors easily enough? Should we have school colours? Unfortunately my term of office finished before we were able to draw up an action plan, but I had set in motion the beginning of what eventually became a parental involvement policy.

Spin-off spiral 1b
Involving the pupils in promoting the school

Making pupils aware that they had an important role in developing and promoting an appropriate image of the school was another strategy that I developed. I have always been keen to involve the pupils and their work in any encounter with parents or the public, as I think it is the best way of demonstrating a quality school (Loftus, 1991). I set about doing this by giving pupils some ownership of the 'quality image' to be presented. My strategy was to involve them in articulating in words and drawings an image of the school based on their perceptions of it as a good school. Over a period of some weeks I visited each class in turn and made a recording of children's answers to two questions: What things do we like about our school? and how can we make our school better? I decided against asking what they did not like because 'a child coming home and discussing good or bad experiences at school with parents, will influence parental opinion' (Harrison and Gill, 1992:116) and I wanted all influences to be positive. My analysis of the data on these tapes gave me tremendous insight into the children's viewpoints. I also asked children to make drawings about what they liked and I used these and some of what they had said to mount a display entitled, 'Why we like our school' in the main foyer for parents and visitors to see. The suggestions made by the children for 'improving their school' were also useful: ideas such as 'pick a crayon off the floor before someone stands on it', and 'pick up coats and hang them up' came from many children. Subsequently, in assemblies I was able to reinforce these ideas and as coats and pencils were picked up off the floor, visitors commented on how good it was to see children looking after their school and on how tidy the school was.

Spin-off spiral 1c
Making an impact on visitors

As I extended my reading about marketing I was struck by the comment, 'You won't get a second chance to make a first impression' (Russell, 1990:6). I wondered what the first impressions for visitors to our school might be? Were they likely to be favourable or unfavourable? These first impressions would certainly play a vital part in prospective parents deciding whether they would choose to send their child to the school or not. The first areas prospective parents saw when entering our school were the car park, the nursery play area and the path leading up to the school. The car park had cans, crisp packets and weeds around the sides; the nursery play area had climbing apparatus which was rusty with paint flaking off and a grass area which was covered in nettles and weeds. The paving slabs which led up to the main entrance of the school had nettles and thistles growing up between them, with ivy which had crept through the adjacent fence making its way across the path.

After a staff discussion of the problem, I consulted the chair of governors to ascertain what could be done and to establish the necessary resources to support subsequent action. I met with the caretaker and toured the site with him, pointing out things I felt could be done in order to improve its presentation. After this we sat in my office and agreed a timetable and discussed resources which would be needed to complete these jobs. I suggested that jobs at the front of the school should have priority because this was where parents and prospective parents would gain their first impressions (Gray, 1989:58).

Over the following weeks the external fabric of the school took on a new look as the following jobs were completed:

- ❑ climbing apparatus was newly painted;
- ❑ all weeds and thistles growing between paved areas around the school were removed;
- ❑ briars growing through the school fence from adjacent land were cut back;
- ❑ overhanging branches were cut so as to make play areas safer;
- ❑ ivy growing across paths was removed;
- ❑ playground markings were re-painted;
- ❑ crisp packets, cans, sweet papers were removed from the school car park;
- ❑ waste area in the nursery complex was cleared of thistles and nettles ready for patchwork paving;
- ❑ sacks of building waste were cleared from our conservation area.

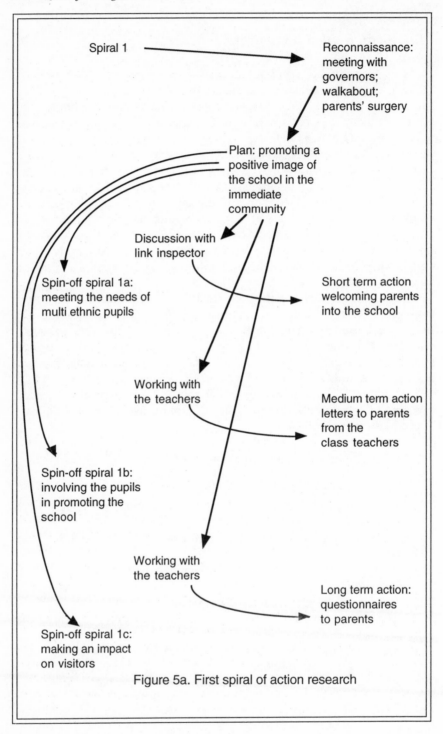

Figure 5a. First spiral of action research

I was extremely pleased with the face-lift given to the school. It was much more presentable and attractive and some potential health and safety issues had been resolved.

During this first cycle of action research I had worked to promote a particular image of the school to the immediate community of parents. I had tried to present a welcoming school, in which the headteacher and staff took a personal interest in the views of its parents and where the pupils were placed at the centre of all activities. I had made an effort to involve teachers and ancillary staff fully in this (the caretaker was now much more motivated and was a person I could count on in the future) and I had made sure that the governors were consulted about the action taken and made aware of the successes achieved. I had also worked with Borough personnel and taken advantage of their expertise. My success in improving communication generally was confirmed by the feedback I was continually receiving from parents, governors and teachers. I was also learning a lot about what 'educational' marketing might look like and developing strategies that I thought would make it succeed. Figure 5a (page 8) shows the main spiral of action which led to a school policy on promoting parental involvement. This involved three main cycles of action: short term, medium term and long term. These actions initiated further spin-off cycles. The first, to do with developing a multicultural curriculum, has not been addressed in this report. The second, to do with involving pupils in developing their image of the school and using their work in its marketing, became a central aspect of the marketing policy. The third involved all members of the school in making it a more attractive place.

Spiral 2
Promoting the school in the wider community

There had been a marked improvement in the way in which we as a school presented ourselves to the parents of our children, and the grounds of the school were neat and tidy and gave a good impression to potential parents. I felt it was time to branch from our immediate school community and to begin to promote the school in the wider community. I began by asking staff and governors to help me do a SWOT analysis: that is to identify Strengths, Weaknesses, Opportunities and Threats for the school. The method is for individuals to write down their ideas in response to a number of set questions. The exercise is commonplace in industry and has a dual function: it identifies areas for development and celebration; but it also raises awareness about issues and encourages people to be more reflective about them. After the SWOT exercise had been completed and I had identified the main issues relevant to marketing the school, I timetabled two staff meetings to develop ideas about possible action. I then met with my governors and followed a similar procedure asking for their ideas and suggestions. I pulled all the ideas together into a marketing policy which we set about trying to implement. (see Figure 5b)

At first school, we are proud of the curriculum we offer to our children. We feel that both the immediate and wider community should be made aware of this.

OUR AIMS ARE:

To encourage parental involvement so that parents may gain a greater understanding of what we are aiming to achieve in the School.

To sustain our enrolment numbers and increase our pupil numbers.

To use additional income outside our budget to improve the quality of education for each child in our school.

To make the community aware of our child-centred approach to education and our commitment to Equal Opportunities with regard to race, sex, class and ability.

To publicise our resources, staff expertise and countrified environment.

To encourage links with industry and the wider community.

To attract potential pupils without sacrificing our school ethos.

To adopt a whole school approach, where teaching staff, ancillary staff and governors accept joint responsibility for marketing our school.

To make sure that all marketing ventures undertaken by our school are to be cost-effective.

The following criteria will be markers for assessing success

1. Has the school increased the numbers of pupils on roll?
2. Is there evidence of improved resourcing?
3   Is there evidence of increased parental involvement?
4. Has School acted on parents' opinions as discovered through the questionnaire replies?
5. Has the marketing policy had a positive effect on the life of the school? If so, where and how?
6. What areas do we need to try harder at?

Figure 5b. A marketing policy for a first school

At these meetings teachers and governors had made a number of practical suggestions about how to implement a marketing policy. At the staff meetings we set about putting these into practice. The following are some of the ways in which we promoted the school in the wider community.

1. We made an effort to target older members of the community. For Harvest Festival we asked parents to donate goods and produce so that we could make up baskets for older persons. Parents were also asked to nominate people who would like to receive these gifts. We also had enough produce left over to auction and the money was given to our local old people's home. At Christmas time we had two Christmas productions at the school to which we encouraged older members of the community to come. We also donated the profits to the local home.

2. We persuaded the local library to display our children's work in the children's section of the library. Two displays were arranged on 'Why we enjoy science' and 'Happy Christmas from a first school'. I knew that many children and their parents/relatives would visit the library at weekends and over the Christmas holidays. They would all see the high standard of our children's work and the name of our school. Hopefully, because of these displays, they might be encouraged to make further enquiries about our school.

3. The proposal for a school-business link was more difficult to arrange because there were few businesses nearby. The only accessible businesses were a parade of shops. The one shop that stood out among the rest was a dry cleaning shop. It was right on the corner of the parade and the name of the shop was in my opinion very effectively displayed in bold yellow letters on a red background. I visited the shop and explained that my school was anxious to make links with its local community, that a link with a business was an important part of the curriculum, and that we would very much like to bring a class of children to visit the shop. They agreed. The visit was a great success; the children accompanied by their teacher and a number of parents were shown how clothes were washed, steam dried, steam pressed and bagged. After the visit the children wrote 'thank you' letters to Mr and Mrs J. I had noticed, whilst visiting, that there was a blank wall in the shop. I suggested that this could be used to display the children's thank you letters and some drawings they had done. The shopkeepers were pleased and impressed by the fact that the children had gone to the trouble o f writing thank you letters and that the school was prepared to display them in his shop.

The children's work was mounted on black sugar paper and displayed on the vacant wall next to the counter. As people were waiting to be served, they could read the thank you letters. Mr and Mrs J were extremely pleased that customers could see how they had helped a school. I was extremely pleased as every letter on show had our school's name and address on it, available for prospective parents and pupils. I was aware that Christmas was coming and this would be a busy time in the shop, meaning even more exposure for the school. I think that Mr and Mrs J had agreed to the children's visit to help the school; the fact that it impressed their customers and maybe enhanced their reputation and sales was a bonus they had not anticipated.

The second spiral of action research had succeeded in involving pupils, teachers and parents in implementing a marketing policy in the wider community that had been developed by staff and governors of the school in response to considerable information gained from parents and pupils. Its implementation had involved bringing the work of the school to the notice of the general public who visited the library and the laundry and specifically to the older members of the community. Figure 5c represents the main spiral of action and shows its relationship to fact finding.

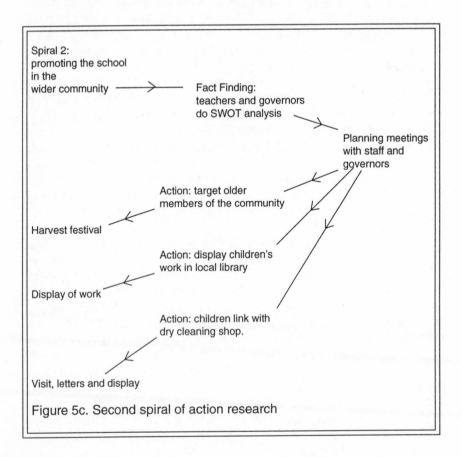

Figure 5c. Second spiral of action research

Conclusion

In reviewing the description and explanation of how I have tried to improve my practice in promoting an appropriate educational image of my school, I realise that I have not only gained a much greater understanding of the sort of educational image that I want to promote, but I have also learned how to collaborate with other members of my school community in developing strategies to market the school that do not conflict with my educational values. For me, the notion of marketing a school no longer conjures up a threatening image of cut-throat competition. Instead I imagine an image of quality schooling that is promoted by the whole community of the school working together. I have reached this position through a number of insights.

I recognise how crucial it was to collaborate closely with my teaching staff, ancillary staff, governors, the inspectorate, parents and the wider community. On analysing the oral and written comments, questionnaires, SWOT pro formas, transcriptions and audio-cassette recordings which I collected during the project, I was able to see the extent to which other people's ideas had informed and influenced my action. All too often headteachers make decisions without consultation so as to save time. I have learned that time saved in this way could be costly in the long run. Besides which, there is an immeasurable advantage to be gained from positively seeking participation with others so that they 'partner' you in bringing about the changes that are required in schools today.

With open enrolment and age weighted pupil numbers under formula funding, children's perceptions are definitely important as these perceptions can influence parental decisions on the choice of school for their child. I intend to continue to seek children's views on why they like their school and on how their school can be improved. I also intend to continue to encourage children to help me present an image of a good school through displaying their work in public.

I have tried to give a readable account of how I executed an action research project of which the main aim was to enhance the image of a first school in the immediate and wider communities. I have learnt a great deal from this project and feel that it has been of enormous benefit to my school. As I have had the good fortune to become the substantive head of my project school, and I am currently oversubscribed, I shall most definitely continue to use the results of this research as a guide to future action.

Chapter 6

Towards a better understanding of changing gender dynamics in a mixed ability classroom

Marian Nicholas

Is the education system merely a reflection of society or does it play a part in shaping patterns of gender relations? Can the school system 'break out' of the gender patterns in society, or is it powerless? There is a considerable range of writing about the construction of sex and gender drawn from biology, psychology and sociology (Lloyd and Archer, 1976; Fox *et al.*, 1977; Sayers, 1987). There are tensions between arguments that emphasise biological difference and those that prefer social explanations. I dispute the passive imprinting theory of gender development and I agree with Anyon (1983) who has argued that gender development for girls is an active response to social contradictions because 'they cope with and resolve contradictory social messages regarding what they should do and be'. Genovese (1983) has called this process 'accommodation and resistance to gender contradictions'. In the research reported in this chapter I worked with Jo (female), the class-teacher of 2B, to intervene in pupils' education to influence their adoption of co-educational forms of interaction.

The tensions between biological and social explanations of gender dynamics in classrooms clearly coloured our feelings about what we set out to do. I prefer to think that gender friendship groups are formed because of similar interest, that is, they are socially rather than biologically determined. This could explain reported hostility between male and female pupils (Clarricoates, 1980; Shave, 1978). On the other hand, Jo was more ambivalent about what she thought. She states on tape, 'Boys are made different from girls ... both boys and girls don't want proximity with the opposite sex .... I think it's natural ... it might be a biological thing ...', yet at the same time she was willing to be prescriptive about putting her pupils into mixed groups for our work together and I think she shared my belief that both boys and girls needed to develop coherent strategies to co-exist intellectually and socially in our classroom.

My job was that of special needs co-ordinator and support teacher. The following enquiry was conducted over two terms in a mixed local authority middle school in an outer London borough. Action research was the methodology used to plan, act, observe and reflect to evaluate classroom practice. The school in the project is located in a densely populated area. There are mixes of social class as well as ethnicity variations, although 80% of pupils in the school have English as their first language. The research was conducted in class 2B. The pupils were 10 years old. There were 29 children in the class, 16 girls and 13 boys. We used teacher judgements to decide the ability of pupils. There were 8 able girls and 3 able boys; 2 boys had statements and there were 2 other boys and one girl with learning difficulties (LD). Three girls and 2 boys spoke English as a second language (ESL).

I have described elsewhere (Nicholas, 1991) how I became conscious of the fact that I had become an example of the concept of living contradiction, negating my educational values in practice (Whitehead, 1993:70) because I failed to offer a curriculum that met the needs of a mixed ability class and I found a 'hidden' sexist curriculum in my classroom. My earlier research described how I sought to bring about changes in the classroom so that discriminatory practices against girls should not continue. An important finding was that group discussions in class enabled teachers to interact more with the girls.

The phase of action research reported in this paper started when I arranged to support Jo, the class teacher of 2B, who wanted to try group discussions in her class. Our work was an attempt at teacher collaborative action research in which we investigated ways to implement a non-sexist classroom within mixed ability teaching to enhance equal opportunity for all pupils. The focus of this paper is twofold: (a) an evaluation of our success in promoting group discussion to enhance the cooperative working of boys and girls in mixed ability groups, and (b) our joint reflections on our own understanding of ourselves as women teachers and how this impinged on the ideal solution to which we were working.

Why use action research?

Action research is a way by which groups of professionals can organise conditions in which they learn from their own experiences. It is a process whereby practitioners can improve their professional competence by analysing the quality of their practice. I like the Kemmis and Henry definition of action research, as 'a form of enquiry undertaken by participants in social (including educational) situations, in order to improve the rationality and justice of their own social or educational practice, their understanding of those practices, and the situations in which the practices are carried out. It is most rationally empowering when undertaken by participants collaboratively' (Kemmis and Henry, 1984). I adopted this model because is seemed simple to use but also because of its explicit commitment to justice and teamwork. Other characteristics of action research that were important to me were a commitment to seek improvement by intervention, a concern to establish a critically reflective approach to our collaboration, a desire to involve the pupils as active participants and an attempt to be rigorous in monitoring outcomes (Forward, 1989).

Based on a process of reflection I hoped that we could develop conversations about our educational practice. This would work at two levels: internal conversations generated when we ourselves observed what was happening in our class and reflected upon it, and public conversations where we would be able to participate in dialogues about imagined solutions and the changes we hoped to implement. Jo's and my internal thinking included our knowledge and feelings about macho-type behaviour in class and school. We were aware when it happened but seldom articulated our dislike of it openly. Public conversations in our study include taped and written documents of conversations. These also acted as evidence for validation and offer explanations and information of the action research. Jo was fully aware of action research methods, from her initial training. This I believe enabled her to understand very quickly, and articulate publicly, what we were attempting to change. Her support to me was invaluable. Who was supporting whom? Certainly at the end of the research period there existed a good situation between us, because we felt that we were developing the pupils within a new form of gender dynamic.

Establishing an understanding of the support role

Before starting the project Jo stated her educational values concerning support teaching. I told her mine. She preferred in-class support rather than the practice of withdrawing children from the class and she saw my role as mainly supporting her, rather than pupils with learning difficulties. She wanted to develop group discussions and thought that in-class support gave more opportunity for this. I believe that a system of two teachers working together in classrooms promotes learning better than a system of withdrawal of pupils from class. Support teaching enables two teachers to plan activities to meet children's needs better than one teacher can. Support teaching allows teachers to share the responsibility of the teaching/learning task. When support teaching has been established, there can be increased communication where openness and discussion and sharing teaching experiences becomes a collaborative activity, and both teachers can learn together from the experience. This view of support teaching is very akin to that of team teaching, but in support teaching one teacher clearly retains responsibility for the class.

I find stating any sort of values difficult. It is quick and easy enough to formulate some educational values, for example about support teaching and whether in-class support is preferable, but from experience I know that implicit values often become clarified during reflection and can make already formulated values inappropriate to the changing context. I believe that this happened as Jo and I developed our action research together. We became like the teachers described by Weiner and Arnot (1987:354) 'trying to be fair to both girls and boys in mixed classrooms ... teachers will find themselves questioning their own preconceived notions of what constitutes good classroom practice in good pupil relations ...'. We subscribe to this because although we always attempted to be fair to all, our initial ideas became questionable as we began to understand the implications of the data we were gathering. For instance, we could not feel justified to continue with our crusade to promote girls exclusively because we observed the ESL boys being marginalised in our classroom.

This led us to see that developing communication/social skills was a major area where we could have the most effect. This thinking was partly covert since we never questioned that we should do this. We saw implicitly that it was an achievable goal and we could effect change of a permanent nature. The ability to discuss, negotiate, make decisions, listen, speak succinctly, is a life-enhancing process for all of us and is, I suggest, part of equal opportunity policies. We wanted to ensure that boys did not take a stereotypical leading role in discussion. Neither did we want ESL pupils or pupils with learning difficulties to feel that they had nothing to offer. It is my considered opinion that this imagined solution offering an androgynous model of interaction suited our gender dynamic perfectly and was successful in promoting all pupils in our class (emphasising similarities rather than differences). On tape Jo says that pupils 'don't have much opportunity to talk and don't know how to talk', which was why she wanted to introduce group discussion in lessons when I supported her.

Clarifying the problem

In order to see what gender dynamics were in place before our team teaching began we decided to count two major categories of interaction between pupils and teacher when Jo worked alone in class. These were pupil-initiated and teacher-initiated ones.

Pupils (Number)	Teacher initiated interactions	Pupil initiated interactions
LD girls (1)	11	3
ESL girls (3)	7	2
Able girls (8)	18	12
All girls (16)	42	17
LD boys (4)	6	8
ESL boys (2)	5	0
Able boys (3)	3	5
All boys (13)	39	37
All pupils (29)	81	54

Figure 6a.
Teacher and pupil initiated interactions in four whole class humanities lessons

The numerical count occurred in whole class lessons and not in group discussions. As a non-participant observer I counted the interactions in four Humanities lessons. The categories I used as a basis for my analysis of these interactions were gender, high ability, learning difficulties (LD), and English as a second language (ESL). For pupil-initiated interactions, the highest score was with boys and the lowest score was with ESL boys. For teacher-initiated interactions, the highest score was with girls and the lowest score was with able boys. We saw that boys dominated conversations when they were the ones initiating the interactions, but in teacher-led interactions Jo was successful in making a positive effort to interact with girls. We also noted that although ESL boys had the lowest pupil-led interaction scores, the ESL girls only initiated two remarks to Jo in four lessons, thus substantiating the point that our problem was not simply one of gender dynamics but of a breakdown in successful mixed ability teaching. Jo was interacting freely with the girls but not with the able boys (three occasions in four lessons only) or the ESL pupils. The girl with learning difficulties (there was only one) had eleven teacher-led interactions but few pupil-initiated interactions. Boys with learning difficulties (there were four) had six (teacher-led) and eight (pupil-led) interactions respectively.

The counting exercise did not provide clear information of the quality of interaction in lessons since it took into account requests such as 'Can I sharpen my pencil, Miss?' and taught us little about how the sexes interacted with each other. Jo and I framed the following questions: What strategies could we use to get all pupils to participate actively in a lesson? How could we maintain our success in ensuring an equal share of teacher-pupil interaction for girls? How could we enhance our pupils' learning within a framework of a non-sexist classroom? Did the pupils understand the concept of sexism?

We agreed that class teaching was likely to result in boys dominating conversation/learning unless the teacher actively worked to ensure that girls were encouraged to participate. In addition, we felt that class teaching was not providing enough opportunity for pupils to engage in meaningful discussion with each other. We saw group interaction as being important for the development of individual pupils' social skills and attitudes to social justice. We were aware that Jo had made a particular effort to interact most with the girls in class discussions but we wanted to ensure that boys would value the girls' contribution. Moreover, we wished to offer mixed ability teaching. So we planned to kill two birds with one interventionist stone, to provide weekly group discussion sessions where girls and boys working in mixed ability groups had the chance to interact with each other under the guidance of teachers. The content of the sessions would consist of group problem solving activities followed by group presentations of solutions. All the problem solving exercises were taken from the book *Ways and Means: An approach to problem solving* produced by the Kingston Friends Workshop Group.

Beginning the group work

One of the reasons why Jo was keen to have me work with her in the classroom was that she wanted to implement group work, which she believed was essential for helping pupils learn to communicate. We agreed that communication with others was an activity which affected all our lives in a deep and fundamental way. From the moment of birth we interact socially. If we tell children that they should be seen and not heard and if children are 'put down' in conversation and if males are allowed to interrupt females constantly and teachers refuse to listen to pupils' views and pupils to teachers', then we are all being undervalued. It was our belief that a consequence of this lack of communication was that a person's self-esteem drops. Pupils need the opportunity to experience affirmation. We believed that if they did not learn to speak in a mixed group, that a potential for the enrichment of their lives and their achievements would be diminished.

Jo placed the pupils in six mixed groupings, ensuring that different genders and abilities were represented in each group and that the ESL children were spread. It was our belief that the group work would be enjoyable and motivating. We predicted that the problem-solving sessions would lead to the emergence of enablers and facilitators amongst the pupils, and they would influence other pupils to contribute. Through this the process of affirmation would be developed and would lead to increased feelings of self-worth and enhanced self-esteem for all the children. Affirmation is an endorsement of what is positive in people. When we are affirmed by others, it gives us a way of evaluating our positive qualities, and its absence confirms our weaknesses. It was our opinion that affirmation was a necessary component for mixed ability teaching because it enables every pupil to have their opinions and ideas valued.

The topics we selected for the group activities were chosen because they reinforced the messages we were trying to introduce through our organisation of teaching and learning in the classroom. The first task we set pupils was to think up ten ways to improve the classroom atmosphere for boys and girls. We audio-taped the class presentation session when each group fed back and listened to each other's solutions to the problem that had been set. All 6 groups said they wanted equality of treatment for girls and boys by the teachers. There was also an emphasis placed on girls and boys sharing and cooperating together. The presentations suggested that the pupils understood the concept of sexism but we were less sure that pupils practised non-sexism in their group discussions. Were they themselves trapped by the concept of being living contradictions, unable to live out in practice their beliefs? Jo and I were grappling with a major problem highlighted throughout the education system, concerning equal opportunities. That is, that everybody appears to understand what equality means and teachers are convinced that they operate equality and teach pupils correct procedures and attitudes of fairness. But is equality really happening? Jo and I were sceptical.

Getting feedback from the pupils

In the second group work session, we applied the same criteria as before and put the pupils into mixed groups, but not necessarily the same groups as before. The problem-solving exercise was to produce a reasoned case for offering a liver transplant when only one liver was available for five individuals. Who had the strongest reasons for being given the liver for survival? After the discussion each group made a presentation to the rest of the class to share their solutions. During these feedback sessions we reinforced the importance of affirmation and of respecting each individual's contribution. At the end of this session we asked every child, individually, to complete an evaluation sheet. This sheet was produced so that all the children would find the task easy to complete.

We asked questions about talking, listening, discussing, leading groups and bossiness. In our analysis of the results we looked for evidence of pupils who had not enjoyed the sessions and evidence of pupils feeling marginalised or feeling dominated by others. Out of the 28 pupils in the class, 21 said that no-one was bossy in the group, 18 claimed that the part of the lesson which they preferred was sharing ideas, 16 said that girls had taken charge of the group, 2 ESL girls and 1 ESL boy said that they had done no talking, and 1 LD girl said that she had not listened.

We were confident from this that boys were not dominating in the group discussion and that girls' opinions and ideas were being valued. However, we were concerned that the three ESL pupils (2 girls and 1 boy) had not talked in the lesson and that one LD boy had not joined in the discussion at the end and the girl with LD had not listened to others. We were still not meeting mixed ability needs because some ability groups were not participating fully. Moreover we had not provided the opportunity for ESL pupils to participate actively. We did not want the ESL pupils under-valuing themselves. Since the data for this analysis was based on questionnaire data and we wanted to confirm the accuracy of what pupils had recorded, we decided to video a lesson and use this as the basis of a further analysis.

Making a video

Videos are valuable forms of documentation since they give opportunities to teachers to see events which they cannot perceive whilst teaching. Teaching is such an all-embracing activity that one does not always know accurately what is happening in class. Videos can crystallise events. We did not relish the thought of seeing ourselves teaching on video, but overcame the fear sufficiently to allow a parent access to video us. It is my opinion that Jo saw the video as a way of appraising her teaching performance and we both saw the video as a way into making our educational practice public.

The lesson we video recorded happened about two months after we had begun the weekly group discussion sessions. We chose a lesson when we were team teaching and agreed to analyse it together afterwards. We hoped the video would show whether children were respected by others, whether they listened to each other, interrupted others, spoke succinctly, felt intimidated, sat in mixed groups, had confidence to speak out, had a fair share of speaking turns. For the lesson that we videoed Jo placed pupils into 5 mixed groups. The task the children were set was to discuss how to survive on a desert island after being shipwrecked.

We hoped the video would help us to evaluate whether we were fostering the educational processes we intended. We wanted to assess whether pupils were operating in a non-sexist way and whether the mixed ability group was functioning successfully. Jo was not sure that we could teach about sexism. Maybe this is true. However, I was clear that we had chosen to focus on gender dynamics and group discussion because we were trying to change sexist attitudes and offer all pupils a chance to be valued.

We watched the video together in order to identify pupil behaviours that supported our analysis, and tape recorded our conversation. Overall we were pleased with the way pupils worked in groups. There was evidence on the video of pupils' motivation and involvement in the work of their groups. There was also evidence that as teachers we had praised the work of four of the groups and been even-handed in the praise we had given to individual boys and girls.

It was interesting that in pupils' solutions to the problem set, stereotypical attitudes were at a minimum; for instance two girls and one boy was prepared to do the cooking and two girls and one boy to go hunting. We looked for interactions showing gender dynamics and evidence of pupils of the opposite sex valuing each other's ideas. There were many examples of boys and girls listening to each other and no examples of either sex putting the other down. Boys were not dominating girls and there was evidence of both boys and girls taking the lead. There was only one example of a pupil interrupting someone of the other sex and that was a boy interrupting a girl, and only one example of a pupil being challenged by someone of the other sex and that was a girl challenging a boy. Both boys and girls acted as spokespersons but there were more examples of boys explaining meaning and more examples of girls acting as scribe, possibly showing a subtle form of stereotyping. There were only two examples of pupils losing confidence, one boy and one girl. We were especially pleased that most girls demonstrated the confidence to speak in a mixed group. On the whole we thought the video demonstrated evidence of real success in having achieved a non-sexist classroom.

The second purpose of analysing the video was to evaluate our success in providing a good learning environment for individual pupils within mixed groups. Only three of the five groups were mixed ability groups. Most of the time the pupils worked as a group although there were examples of this not happening. For example Jo was critical of the mix of pupils she had established in one group, remarking, 'Christopher is obviously switched off the task. He sees himself as doing all the work. Look at him – he's acting as scribe and contributing most of the ideas to solve the problem.'

The spokespersons for the groups were spread across the ability range. There were many examples of able boys and girls contributing to the work of the groups, although there was one example of an able girl losing confidence. There was evidence that the ideas of pupils with learning difficulties were affirmed and that all of them had contributed and had listened. There was evidence that all the ESL children were actively listening but not all of them had contributed to the discussion and there was one example of two ESL boys taking the opportunity to play up to the camera.

Jo also watched the video with her class and discussed with them how they had interacted with each other. She commented, 'I asked the class to look out for occasions when they interrupted others. They didn't find many. We discussed how they worked in a group ... three-quarters of the group thought they had.'

Evaluating intervention

Did we find an optimum way of organising class 2B so that equality of opportunity existed for the majority of pupils? We believed that offering group discussions had brought about improvements in the way that pupils interacted with each other.

Informal feedback from parents to Jo was already suggesting a spin-off outcome in that some parents had commented that their children were starting to give extended answers rather than yes/no answers. Our original belief that group work was an essential element in the curriculum and that whole class discussions were not the best way of promoting the participation of all pupils was confirmed. We had reached some tentative conclusions about grouping pupils. We decided that it was best to put the five ESL pupils in two groups so that they could give each other confidence, but not necessarily put the two boys together. Since one girl was both 'able' and ESL, she could represent either an 'able' pupil or an ESL pupil in the group mix. The two boys with statements could also support each other in one group as they had shown themselves doing on the video. The other pupils with LD and the able boys and girls should be shared amongst the groups with at least one able girl or boy in each group. This meant one group would be top heavy with able pupils. We agreed that strict monitoring of groups was advisable on a weekly/daily basis and that groups should be changed periodically so that pupils could work with a wide variety of other children.

At the start of the intervention I had put in place a strategy to evaluate the outcomes in terms of changes in pupils' self-esteem. My own belief is that making claims about change is enhanced by quantitative analysis. I had searched for a standardised test that would show change in pupils' attitudes to the issues we were addressing. It proved difficult to find what I wanted, but I discovered a test which assessed changes in self-esteem. This is the Lawseq questionnaire (Lawrence, 1988:15) which has been standardised on both an English and an Australian population. Since we were aiming to affirm pupils during the project and hoping for improvement in self-esteem, especially in girls and ESL pupils, I felt this test was appropriate.

> The Lawseq questionnaire was administered to the pupils in class 2b before and after our intervention in the curriculum. When testing for difference in the pre and post test results I used the Wilcoxon Signed Ranks Test for difference between pairs. The result was significant at $p < .05$ and on the basis of these results it could be claimed that there was a significant improvement in self-esteem in the pupils in class 2B over the period of our intervention.

Evaluating our own learning

Weiner and Arnot (1987:354) said that little attention has been paid to the personal and professional implications for teachers as agents of change when they challenge traditional sexual divisions in schooling. It is important not to underestimate the enormity of the target we set ourselves. It was difficult, lengthy and time consuming. Others have described such classrooms (Spender, 1982; Randall, 1987; Stanworth, 1987) and the difficulty of changing their dynamics should not be underestimated. I have already noted Jo's ambivalence about how far she felt she could intervene to change gender dynamics. On tape she says, 'It's not even anybody's fault ... women have got used to thinking that they should rush home from work and cook and clean ... while the husband can come in ... mow a lawn and that's it ...' Yet she saw herself developing a different model of gender dynamics in her classroom that was succeeding, one based on mixed gender group work and the teacher being non-sexist and through reading books like *The Paper Bag Princess* and through drama; a model to be built upon in future years so that when she says to pupils to get into groups 'they wouldn't dream of going into single sex groups ...'.

An important dimension of our work which we recognised and talked about was our commitment to the ideal and the way that this was coloured by negative feelings within ourselves about our gender and our low self-esteem as women. Jo expressed this feeling clearly despite being aged nine when the Sex Discrimination Act became law and feeling that her generation could probably bring about changes. My achievements had been influenced by being female. For example, my parents did not want me to go on to university because they thought that, like other girls, I would get married and waste all the resources that had been used on my education. Implicit in this view was the assumption that girls would not work outside the home after marriage. It was difficult for me to comprehend this idea since my mother worked in factories all her life. Eventually my parents allowed me to do a teacher training course and I have been in paid employment for 30+ years since I first qualified as a teacher in 1954.

Problems are apparent in my career structure too. Working in male dominated management organisations such as London schools has not contributed to developing high self-esteem. I will mention a few brief points about my career structure. In 1954 women teachers were paid less than men doing the same job. This was my first encounter with inequality in the work place. Living in a male-dominated society and becoming a mother in 1961 and 1963 forced me to do either no teaching or part-time work for a number of years, since there were no adequate child facilities available. I became a scale two teacher in full-time employment in 1970, but this post disappeared when the main professional grade was implemented. Some of my low self-esteem is linked to feelings of low status in my professional work. At the same time my unpaid labour in the domestic sphere was considerable. Like many other women (Oakley, 1990), I have worked between 12 and 14 hours a day during the school week. It is difficult with a history like this to be very positive about my gender. In other words, I feel under-valued.

There are shades of a 'living contradiction' here where Jo and I as female teachers were attempting to promote girls despite our own perspective of low-esteem about our gender identity. This is what I meant earlier about personal feelings sometimes being difficult to reconcile with stated values. Stating educational values is seen as a benchmark and used as a criterion for the purposes of assessing personal development in action research. For instance, Whitehead said that we are motivated to improve when we see ourselves denying our values in our actions. He said, 'I give the reasons for why I do things in terms of the values I hold as I try to overcome my experience of their negation' (Whitehead and Lomax, 1987:184). Does this imply that values are unchanging and unproblematic? That it is practice alone that is problematic? I think that as Jo and I became clearer about our own gendered understandings through exploring our practice in trying to help pupils, our original stated educational values about support teaching shifted. Whitehorn (1991) says that 'no-one studies anything without bringing to it a whole construct of their own values, culture, upbringing ...'. This may be true, but it is through studying that we can come to understand this 'whole construct' and in doing so perhaps change what it means. How far, therefore, could we be successful in promoting girls to think positively about themselves, when Jo and I brought low-esteem about our gender identity to this project? We cannot answer this question and neither can the research. Fortunately, there is a converse feeling about gender and that is the resistance theory where girls/women who feel oppressed by the system can offer resistance (McRobbie, 1978; Wallace, 1987). It seems that Jo and I subscribed to this theory in spite of low self-esteem since we were committed to developing equal chances for girls. This was probably due to a professional commitment, where our personal feelings became subsumed in our search to become agents of change. In other words, if the Sex Discrimination Act (1975) is the official commitment to making society more equal, what we tried to do in this small study can be seen in the spirit of trying to implement the Act!

Chapter 7

Preparing student teachers to respond to special educational needs: science boxes for children being taught at home or in hospital

Di Hannon

In this paper I describe a curriculum initiative whereby first year science teacher training students prepared science boxes for children who were being taught at home or in hospital. A 'science box' is a portable self-contained resource box containing science activities and materials matched to part of the science national curriculum and sufficiently flexible to use in a variety of teaching situations. The intention behind the initiative was to give student teachers experience of preparing science work for primary school children and at the same time to promote their understanding of the needs of pupils with a range of physical and sensory special needs. I used an action research approach to develop the research. In what follows I hope to share the motivation, commitment and excitement of developing work along these lines and provide data to support my claims that I have implemented a science education programme that not only gave students a valuable educational experience but also produced a portable resource that is being tried out for more general use by home and hospital tutors.

The Home and Hospital Teaching Service (HHTS)

The 1993 Education Act placed a statutory duty on local education authorities to provide a suitable education for children who were out of school for reasons of sickness. The role of education in hospital has been described as ' ... offering stimulation and a recognisable link to normal life, helping to reduce the child's stress and helping to maintain the academic process' (Wilson, 1993:24). Wiles (1988:160) says that when questioned 'the majority of hospital teachers said that they liked hospital teaching because they felt they had provided normality for the children'. The Home and Hospital Teaching Service (HHTS) gives tuition to children who are unable to attend school because of illness. The tutors not only teach across the curriculum, but adapt work for a variety of different ages and needs. The tuition may take place in hospital classrooms, hospital wards or at home. Although many of the children who have been taught out of school return to mainstream education and break their links with the HHTS, others may need to be taught on a regular basis because their attendance at school is intermittent due to their particular condition.

Traditionally much of the teaching of sick children has concentrated on language and mathematics and only relatively recently has there been a move to include science (Baggaley, 1992). This has been partly due to the national curriculum [1] which has legislated that science is taught as part of the core curriculum in the primary school. Although the national curriculum is not mandatory in hospital schools, the Department for Education has advised that 'hospital teachers should try to provide a broad and balanced curriculum complementary and comparable to that in main stream schools' (DFE, 1994). Kibby (1989:22-23) sums up the situation: 'Children in hospital as a transient population must not be disadvantaged by exclusion from the national curriculum and teaching in hospital cannot be divorced from the attainment levels and programmes of study being followed in mainstream school'. These declarations, however, are of no value unless provision is made for adequate programmes to happen. There are some examples of good practice such as the Hospital Schools Science Research Project which has attempted to broaden provision so that pupils were able to follow a science curriculum (Dewsbury and Jones, 1984). However, in the particular circumstances of home and hospital teaching, science equipment and organisation may present problems. Also, as in mainstream teaching, teachers who have not had a background of science training themselves may lack some confidence.

As part of my role as a science tutor to the B.Ed. course I must introduce students to knowledge of science and prepare them to teach science to primary school children in order to meet the national curriculum requirements. I also aim to generate enthusiasm for the subject which will communicate itself through student teachers' own teaching, together with a real appreciation of the differing needs of individual pupils. I believe that the science component of the initial training of teachers can play an important part in ensuring that teachers are equipped to help children with special educational needs. In the work described in this paper my aim was to satisfy this dual challenge, of helping students to prepare for teaching the science national curriculum while at the same time promoting their awareness of a range of disabilities that required them to differentiate that curriculum. Because of contact with the HHTS, I was able to draw on their expertise and use their situation for the work. This led to an additional outcome, of doing something practical to help the education of children at home or in hospital. Figure 7a is an overview of the main parts of the project.

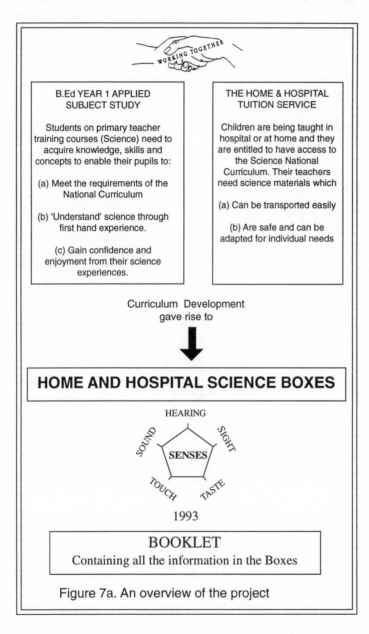

Figure 7a. An overview of the project

The importance of understanding disability

Although society has made strides to integrate people with disabilities, there is still a lack of understanding and fear of disability that my work in science with teacher training students could influence. I have associated my work in this area with the slogan 'Does he take sugar?' science (derived from the title of a radio programme which emphasised how many of us take for granted that a person with disability cannot communicate normally). As teachers, we often lack understanding of how disabilities can impair children's work in classrooms. Broken arms and asthma, for example, are very familiar in primary schools, but this is not always accompanied by complete understanding by the other pupils or the teachers. One of my students who went to a special school where the majority of boys had asthma wrote, 'Many people still do not understand how dangerous it is to push children with asthma to do exercise when they are not feeling well'. Another example is that of a child with asthma who was placed near a chalk board, possibly leading to aggravation of the condition by dust. These anecdotes illustrate the importance of ensuring that teachers have practical knowledge to deal with such situations. This has been recognised by the 1994 Code of Practice (DFE, 1994) on the identification and assessment of special educational needs which requires class teachers to provide data for stage one of the assessment process. This means that students leaving teacher training courses will need to be clear about their responsibilities and competent in dealing with special needs.

The methodology of the study

I have drawn upon an action research perspective to highlight the educational nature of my research and to provide a disciplined methodology for evaluating the action. McNiff (1988:10-20) contrasts action research with traditional ways of conducting research in education 'based on a method which tries to quantify, as if people are entirely predictable', whereas 'action research attempts to make sense of situations from a completely different stand. If (the traditional) method views its functions as problem solving, then action research may be seen as problem posing'. I would not claim that I identified a problem, but I did identify what I perceived to be a need and a challenge. This was more in line with the view that action research starts from a concern to which we imagine a solution and can work towards implementing that solution (Whitehead, 1993:54). My concern was that the student teachers in my science classes should be able to differentiate their science teaching to take account of children with different 'disabilities'. My action research was similar to that which is directed at improving teaching so that as teachers we can live out our clearly articulated educational values in informed committed action (Lomax, 1994b:159).

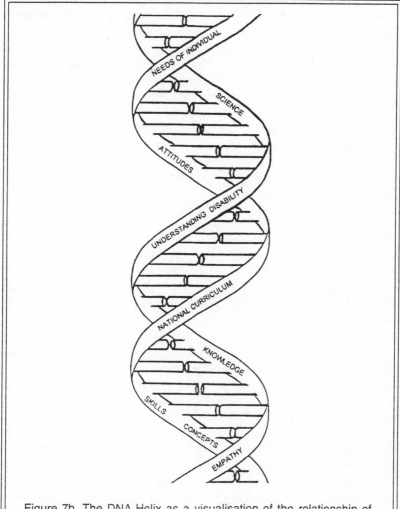

Figure 7b. The DNA Helix as a visualisation of the relationship of teaching national curriculum science and promoting an awareness of the need to understand disability.

I sought to incorporate an element which had previously not existed in any deliberate and defined way in my science teaching. Over recent years I have become increasingly aware of the need for a greater understanding of disability. In some preliminary, unpublished research, I asked a group of 30 teachers to identify disabilities in their mainstream schools. They identified no fewer than 49 different disabilities! In the same way that every teacher should be a teacher of language, mathematics and health education, I would add understanding disability. As a science tutor this was my starting point from which I began my first cycle of action research: I made a plan, carried out the action, monitored my action, evaluated the outcome and attempted to validate my conclusions. Following Lomax and Parker (1995) I have attempted to visualise my action research in a way which makes sense of it to me. Figure 7b shows this visualisation as a double helix which highlights the connection I have attempted to make between the teaching of science and the promotion of awareness of disability.

My general plan was to incorporate an element of 'understanding disability' into my science teaching for Year 1 B.Ed. students so that this philosophy would underpin the next three years of the four year teacher training programme. The action plan I chose was to develop science boxes for the HHTS. I was pleased with this idea because it was an exciting new development yet compatible with techniques I had used previously. I enjoy working with students whereby they have a challenge which leads to a specific outcome. In the past these outcomes may have been a teaching kit, a presentation, an interactive display, a set of teaching materials or, on one occasion, a contribution to a primary science book. This can help students to value their own work. Science boxes were another variation of this approach.

There were a number of issues that I needed to address. If the boxes were to be used in a different teaching situation, how could I prepare students for a situation that was different from the teaching they had witnessed in school? Would students be sufficiently motivated for the eventual 'sacrifice' of parting with their teaching materials to the hospital? If students did not keep the boxes, how could they use their work again? Once the students had completed the design and construction of the science boxes, how could I evaluate if students' understanding of science and disability had been enhanced? Would the boxes be useful to home and hospital tutors? I wanted to know if there had been an equal opportunities outcome for physically or sensory impaired children in terms of their science education. I realise that these questions are linked to the issue of validating action research and that such validation takes a different form to that found in scientific and traditional social science research (Lomax, 1994d).

As a 'beginning' action researcher my claims are tentative.

1. I think that the work described has helped to clarify for me, and for my students, a broader view of science education than we previously held. We have begun to understand better the needs of children with certain kinds of disability.
2. I am convinced that the students had a valuable educational experience and that they have glimpsed a vision of their potential as teachers who

can differentiate their science teaching to give pupils with a range of disabilities access to a science education.

3. We have designed a science resource that has been welcomed by the HHTS and is being promoted by the National Association for the Education of Sick Children (NAESC) so that I have been able to set up trials of a new edition of a science box in 50 contexts across the UK.

Working with the students

I had the opportunity to carry out my research within a ten hour course unit *Ourselves and Other Animals*, which I teach to year one B.Ed. students. The broad aims and objectives of this part of the university science course are

1. to relate the selection of content and task design to pupils' levels of cognitive development,
2. to provide learning experiences for a range of abilities, and
3. to recognise the importance of social interaction and co-operation in children's learning in science and technology.

It seemed to me that the preparation of science boxes for home and hospital tutors would meet these objectives. I decided on the topic of 'the senses' as an appropriate choice as it provided easily identifiable opportunities for students to empathise with impairment of one of the senses. I began by dividing students into five groups, each group to focus on one of the five senses. They were required to prepare activities with guidance for the teacher and recording ideas for children with specific individual needs. This was a demanding challenge for the students after just one term at the university and I was aware that I had to devise ways of developing my students' understanding of the issues.

I was fortunate in making contact with the head of the HHTS in SE and SW Surrey. She generously gave time to contribute an initial input, giving the students the context for their project and an appreciation of its importance in contributing to the science education of children in these circumstances. Her talk created great interest and motivation and she was able to establish that if the boxes were successful they would be used by tutors working with children being taught in hospital or at home. A comment from one of the students in the final evaluation questionnaire summed up the reaction of most of the students: 'I was very motivated by the fact that the boxes were going to be of use and help in a real situation.'

The students were then asked to create an opportunity to enhance their own understanding of a particular temporary or permanent physical need. They devised their own ideas for empathising with a disability themselves or interviewing someone well known to them such as a brother, sister, parent or relative. It was interesting that one student found it possible to impair her sense of taste whilst another described how her own life was affected by the lack of a sense of smell. They all wrote about their problems, solutions and feelings. Their readiness to share these experiences, in discussion, within our group was a fascinating input. Such personal involvement gave a commitment and appreciation of the restrictions and a real insight into what it was like to have, for example, partial sight, partial hearing, a broken arm or some other physical challenge. One student summed up the general experience: 'I concluded that doing most things was still possible but much more time consuming and required much more effort.'

After the enlightenment of this empathetic experience the students worked in groups to develop their own scientific knowledge of one of the sense organs and then imaginatively to create a series of multi-sensory experiences through activities designed to help pupils with different needs to find out more about one of the senses. The importance for all children to be given first hand experiences and an opportunity to investigate is constant whether children are being taught at home, school or hospital, and the boxes were intended to help achieve this goal. The students were given a list of criteria (devised by myself and my colleague from the HHTS) to help plan and select the contents of their box. Figure 7c lists these criteria.

There should be:

☐ evidence that the work in the box is related to the national curriculum science;

☐ a high standard of presentation of materials for the science based activities;

☐ guidance for the pupil and the teacher to indicate the purpose of the activity and how it is carried out;

☐ a variety of recording ideas for children within their various limitations;

☐ potential for extension of science;

☐ potential for cross curricular work;

☐ information on the sense organ concerned;

☐ a resources list;

☐ an opportunity to empathise with the special needs associated with impairment of one sense based on the student's own empathising activities.

Figure 7c Criteria for selecting materials for the science boxes

---

The completed boxes

The boxes on the five senses were designed, completed and filled with activities, models, teaching materials, work cards for children and notes for the teacher. Part of the strength of the set of boxes as a teaching resource was the variety of materials and approaches. The 'sense of touch box' was lined with lovely red furry material and contained a variety of man-made and natural materials of varying shapes and textures for sorting, classifying, testing and considering temperature differences, together with a rich selection of animal 'feeler' pictures and recording ideas and notes for the teacher. In one of the other boxes which contained food pictures the student had managed to get the words written in braille for partially sighted pupils so there was the opportunity to cross link materials between the boxes. The students who designed the 'sounds like fun box' wanted it to help children understand how sound was made, travels and how we and other animals hear it. A beautifully made varnished balsa wood sound box, with a length of rubber band that could be altered, was intended to help understand pitch and how a sound could be altered. A tape recording 'recognising noises in the home' was intended to stimulate investigation of how sounds are made, used and heard, *via home made eardrums!* At the end of an activity involving listening to a sound tape, the pupil is asked to 'think about the sounds around you' and 'why not blindfold yourself and listen carefully – you may hear sounds you have never heard before!'. I was pleased to see, in the teachers' notes, a sensitive message: 'if a child has sight impairment avoid playing the above message after the eight noises'.

Many of the students had tried to apply their understanding of individual disabilities in this way. Their activities in the boxes were bright and attractive to sick children and incorporated a range of science activities and recording methods accessible to children with different types of disability. Some of the teaching materials were made waterproof for hygienic reasons. Others gave children, who could not write easily, an opportunity to place their responses by adhering labels or pictures by velcro. For example, the fabric samples provided for sorting activities on a folding felt board could be positioned with velcro so that a child could work with the board placed vertically if necessary. Students also differed in their solutions to particular problems, so that one student, as a result of empathising with a broken arm, decided not to use velcro because 'it is impossible to remove velcro from a mobile background with only one hand! I decided that my activity had to use card pieces that could easily slide into position using only one hand'.

The boxes were prepared so that teachers had easy access to the relevant subject matter, ideas for presenting and recording material and the necessary equipment. The boxes were intended for use in home and hospital teaching in a variety of ways and in a variety of circumstances. In the case of children on a short visit to hospital, a tutor could select an appropriate item to generate interest and motivate a pupil to feel some sense of achievement in the short time available. In the case of children who spend longer periods of hospitalisation (such as children with cystic fibrosis who visit hospital on a regular basis) a tutor would be able to plan a progression of work from the selection of materials available. Similarly tutors in the HHTS deal with children who may be taught at home for prolonged spells, for example as with some cases of chronic fatigue syndrome or school exclusion. They, too, could transport a self-contained package to their pupils.

Evaluating the students' learning

It is too early to ascertain the long term impact of this experiment on student learning, either in relation to differentiating work in primary science or to enhanced understanding of individual needs in science teaching. There is little doubt about the quality of students' work, and this had external verification when a report of the work won a commendation in the 1994 Commonwealth Association for Science, Technology and Mathematics Educators (CASTME) annual awards. I asked the students to complete a questionnaire to give their perception of the new skills, concepts and knowledge they had acquired. All 25 students completed this questionnaire. The responses identified new practical skills that had been learnt such as laminating, making overlays, working with balsa wood. They also identified an enhancement of their own science education, including a better understanding of the science national curriculum. They claimed to be better at writing rationales, laying out work cards, making topic webs and putting together a science topic for teaching. A number of students highlighted the value of group work for sharing skills and experience and setting a higher overall standard. The personal benefits were many and varied; one student said, 'I have learned a lot from this whole assignment, from co-operating with others, study skills and presentation to empathy. I was very motivated by the fact that the boxes were going to be of use and help in a particular situation.' Another remarked, 'I should like to become an empowering teacher of all children regardless of their personal circumstances' – and this seemed a good philosophy on which to base future teaching [2].

Evaluating the science boxes

The nature of the work undertaken by the HHTS means that only a few materials are selected at a time as seems appropriate for the education of a particular child. This means that it will be a long time before many of the materials are used with children. This, of course, is the intention of the boxes so that tutors can choose for specific individual needs. Sometimes children are in and out of hospital, sometimes they are not well enough to undertake the planned work and this is why materials that are flexible and can be utilised as appropriate can provide an additional science resource. Two months after beginning to use a science box, a tutor from the HHTS was invited to speak about her work at a Kingston Conference. In her talk she had this to say about the box: 'useful for a broad age range covering a wide ability range so coping with physical and cognitive challenges. They were compact, portable and easy to store. The work was relevant to the national curriculum but with cross curricular potential and this was useful.' She went on to suggest that a problem was that the materials were not necessarily durable and in time would need to be replaced and that there were not enough boxes available!

Most of the evaluative data currently available comes from the occasion when the boxes were handed over to the hospital tutors, and is in the form of photographs of hospitalised children working with the materials. Walker (1993) suggests that photographs can constitute the main data of evaluation and research, though as evidence, they are strengthened by other data from interviewing, observations, displays and discussion. The photographs that were taken captured hospitalised children's first reactions to the science materials, and provide some evidence of motivation and interest, albeit on a very short time scale. Children who are unwell may not feel motivated to work and have limited powers of concentration. Photographs are inevitably static and so cannot in themselves provide evidence of concentration span but they can give some indication of level of interest, which is so crucial to the success of the science activity. Photographs in the archive capture moments such as an older pupil and a hospital tutor working out how sound travels, with both obviously enjoying using a home-made pot telephone; the fascination on the face of a pupil as a student explains the selection of items in the display of the contents of the 'Sounds Like Fun' box; the animated faces of a student teacher and a hospital tutor as they discuss the use of sounds in a 'sounds in the home' tape recording; a hospital tutor completely absorbed watching for the response of a child to the lovely smooth wooden shapes being held to her cheek. The two photographs chosen to illustrate the work are from a sequence which shows an activity of matching the correct nose to an animal. Figure 7d captures the student explaining the purpose of the activity. Figure 7e captures the concentration on the child's face as he works on his own.

Figure 7d. A student teacher explaining to a hospitalised child the purpose of activities related to the sense of smell.

Figure 7e. A child fully engrossed with an activity to do with the sense of smell.

Current action to evaluate the boxes

One of the problems of evaluating the effectiveness of this work as a way of supporting individual needs in different situations, is the problem of conducting adequate field trials. Fortunately the potential of the original science boxes was recognised by the director of the National Association for the Education of Sick Children and she has been instrumental in commissioning fifty pilot boxes of one of the later prototype boxes to try out in the field. This opportunity has provided the impetus to seek funding for the research and this has been successful in a bid to the Nuffield Foundation. The research seems particularly appropriate at this time when the need for continuity in education for sick or injured children, whether at home or in a hospital, has been recognised in the joint DFE/NHS Circular 12/94 and the revised national curriculum which 'provides teachers with much greater flexibility to respond to the needs of pupils with identified special education needs'(DFE, 1995).

The field trial will enable me to answer some of the unanswered questions that were posed at the beginning of this paper. It will also provide an opportunity to involve some of the original student researchers in the work at a later stage in their B.Ed. programme. I hope that through adopting this teaching strategy in part of the B.Ed. we can help potential teachers to advance the cause of equal opportunities by enabling all children to have equal access to the science curriculum. I was pleased to see the following reaction from one of the student teachers in her completed evaluation questionnaire. She wrote that she had found, 'surprisingly, that sick children are very little different from well children when it comes to learning' – *that is* when suitable resources have been provided.

NOTES

(1) The national curriculum applies to pupils of complusory school age and is organised on the basis of four key stages. The key stages pertinent to primary aged children are key stage 1 (5-7 year olds) and key stage 2 (7-11 year olds). Science is one of the core subjects alongside mathematics and English and, as for each subject and for each key stage, the programmes of study set out what pupils should be taught.

(2) The students were tremendously generous of their time and effort. Most went well beyond the normal statutory requirements of the University course. Although the materials went to the hospitals concerned a booklet was collated for the students so that they had their own concrete record of their achievements. This book is also in demand from other interested parties.

Chapter 8

Using story as a method of facilitating staff development in a secondary school department

Moyra Evans

I have been working in my school to establish a collaborative community of novice action researchers who have used story to explore their own concerns about their teaching or management practice. This has been successful and it has been shown elsewhere how teachers claim that not only has their practice changed as a result of the process, but they have also developed and changed as people seeing their work and working relationships differently (Evans, 1993, 1995a; Pimenoff, 1995). In this paper I explain how I first came to use story as a means of helping teachers develop their work.

Working within an action research perspective, I had supported one of the departments at Roseacre School for a period of one year, during which time we met together on a weekly, timetabled basis for inservice sessions. The department was finding that one of its major values, that of enabling pupils to achieve the highest qualifications of which they were capable, was being denied in its practice. A study of the GCSE results showed that, where students were gaining a majority of A-C grades in other subjects, they were not doing so in the particular subject for which the Department was responsible. When we began to look in detail at departmental perceptions, it became clear that a fundamental review of what was happening in the classrooms was needed. So I talked through with Harriet, who was the head of the department, the sort of issues which we could look at as a department, and one period each week was set aside for all members of the department to meet together, led by Harriet, and supported by me, the deputy headteacher responsible for staff development.

At first I found it hard just to get on the inside of teachers' thinking and experiences. I ascertained that some of the department were happy for me to go into their classrooms, so I was able to pick up quite a lot of what was happening from what I observed. I also became more conversant with the methodology through which they delivered their programmes of study, and could empathise with them over some of the evident problems. I struggled to find solutions; I listened to them a lot and I worried that they would expect me to provide them with answers. I realised that I could help them to talk about and analyse their situations, to reflect on their experiences, to apply theory and empirical evidence when appropriate, to verbalise insights into their practice, and to share, try out and report upon new ideas. Throughout this time, I worked with Harriet to help her understand what was required of her as the leader of the group, and how she could draw her colleagues along with her.

The year's INSET provided me with a lot of data which I was unsure how to use. I had collected data through my diary, my INSET log book, audio-tapes, reports written by the department on lessons, reports written by the head of department on the general progress at points during the year, and the evaluation forms which I asked my colleagues to fill in at the end of the summer term. I had been clear about my agenda but was unsure about my success. I had tried to enable Harriet to lead her department in such a way as to help them to be successful. I had been anxious that the department should take control of their own learning through researching their practice, seeing where improvements were necessary, and planning their own improvements. I had wanted to make the programme useful for the department, so that they would feel better about their teaching and the children would be able to learn more effectively.

I had a wealth of data through which I could describe the events of the year but I was seeking a way of moving from a description to an explanation of my practice, a way of grounding theory in the real events of what had happened. At this time I read about fictional-critical writing as a method for educational research. One idea was to write a story 'that would respond to and organise the data previously collected' (Winter, 1991:261). The attraction of the fictional form, according to Walker (1981:163) was that it offered 'a licence to go beyond what, as an evaluator/ researcher, you can be fairly sure of knowing'. The story would be given to others to read and they could use their own insights and experience to help me 'learn from the data ... (and) ... be responsive and sensitive to what is new and surprising in it' (Winter, 1991:252). Winter stressed that 'theory cannot simply be derived from data, but is always the outcome of a process in which researchers must explore, organise, and integrate their own and other's theoretical resources as an interpretive response to data' (op.cit.: 261). The advantage of the story was that it could represent the discontinuities and tensions in the data and convey 'ambiguity, complexity, and ironic relationships between multiple viewpoints' (Winter, 1991:252).

I drew up a narrative called *The Canterbury Tales*. It was made up of a number of different stories about different individuals in Department A and their response to the INSET sessions as I imagined them. I found that it enabled me to distance myself emotionally from the scene of the research. It was also a way of protecting my colleagues whose names and identities I changed, whilst enabling me to 'go public' to test my explanations of what had happened. For me, as an action researcher who had lived for twelve months both with the problems and with the colleagues who struggled daily with them, this was a very significant advantage.

The writing of the stories helped me to gain new insights into the attitudes, values and ways of thinking of each character, and the relationships within the group, and therefore the problems that they had faced. In this sense the writing itself created an inner tension that enabled me to take a number of apparently contradictory elements and synthesise them into a new understanding – what Lomax and Parker (1995) called the intra-subjective dialectic of action research, where we can develop our own understanding through a dialogue with the representation we are creating. I was also able to organise my data in an interesting way, making it more inviting for people to read, so that I could give it to others to read and ask for their comments. These comments moved my understanding further so that I was able to think more creatively about the support that the school could give its teachers. For me, the writing of the stories, the feedback I got about the stories and the discussions in which I engaged as a result of these stories was a tremendously educational experience, enabling me to move from description to explanation of the staff development issue. Unfortunately this learning was not shared with the people whose discussions and actions had generated the data upon which the stories were based and I became very aware that in not giving back the stories to the teachers, which for several reasons I felt I could not, I was depriving them of an educational experience.

I became aware of the work of Carter and Doyle, 1987; Carter, 1990; and Carter and Gonzales, 1990, and this moved me to other possibilities of using story as part of staff development. Carter had used student teachers' 'well remembered events' as stories told in order to make sense of their experiences. She said that experienced teachers have a rich store of situated stories or storied knowledge from which to draw when deciding on a course of action and that expertise in teaching was dependent on acquiring 'event structured knowledge' (Carter, 1993:7). I began to think that there was an opportunity to create stories which could be shared with experienced colleagues, and which would include aspects of theory, the relevance of which teachers often fail to see. I imagined that stories could be the means of helping teachers challenge their own everyday perceptions so as to be able to step back from them and see them in a different light, and engage in what Schön (1983:165) called 'reframing'. I thought that these stories could include events set in the familiar context of our own school and so incorporate values, attitudes and culture which were so important to us. My excitement at the possibility of using story in a creative way was related to my strong feeling that I would like teachers' knowledge to be more widely shared in schools, to be accessible in its language, and to be captivating for its audience.

The six teachers in Department A were due to meet fortnightly for inservice sessions. I decided to experiment and write a story for them. The story I wrote was called *Darren*. It was a fictionalised account of real events that I had experienced but it incorporated dilemmas which I perceived to be of particular concern to them. There were three main elements in the story. The central element was the character Darren. Each year I commented on the students' records of achievements and saw a limited number of students to talk about their progress. I frequently talked to them about their classroom behaviour if it had been highlighted as needing improvement. Darren was an amalgam of some of these children. The second element was the context in which Darren misbehaved. I had read many reports from Department A which said something similar to this comment: 'Darren must apply himself more conscientiously to this subject. He needs to understand that he will not achieve his potential unless he behaves in a more mature manner in class and begins to take his studies seriously'. Often Department A's remark would be the least good of all eight reports in any one Record of Achievement. The third element was my own role in relation to supporting staff. I wished to question whether this was appropriate and whether the teachers thought that our INSET sessions were helpful.

Apart from the three main elements in the story, it also contained a number of unresolved dilemmas which I have marked in the story in footnotes. These dilemmas were:

❐   The students often claimed they couldn't do the work, but the teachers, in conversation with me, would say that they could do it if only they would try harder.   D1

❐   The students appeared pleasant and sensible in my room, but my experience of calling in on the classroom unannounced confirmed that they could be entirely different, and sometimes totally unsatisfactory in the lessons.   D2

❐   The students often took the easy way out of promising to improve. Sometimes I think they meant it, but it was a different matter when it came to the actual demands of the classroom. They often failed to keep their promises.   D3

❏   I intended to follow up the students' progress, but pressure of other commitments often made this difficult to do.   D4

❏   While I was quite happy to talk to teachers about students, this should really have been the support role of the head of department, who was closer to the scene, and was the manager of 'the team'.   D5

❏   I knew from listening and observing that bad behaviour in class happened. How could teachers be helped to improve the situation? Were there things we had not tried?   D6

When I gave the story to the department I did not acknowledge these dilemmas as I wanted my colleagues to use the story heuristically. My purpose was that the story should act as a catalyst for discussion, but I hoped that it might spur my colleagues to write their own stories, and that in so doing they would be exploring their own practice and making discoveries about it.

The Story of Darren

'Come in, Darren!' called Kate to the youth at the door. 'Have you brought your report with you?'

'Oh no, Miss. I didn't realise you wanted that.'

'Since I asked you here to discuss it, you would have been well advised to bring it along with you. Didn't your form tutor tell you to bring it?'

'Yes, but I never thought about it till this morning. It's at home, Miss.'

'Hmm' replied Kate, distinctly displeased. 'Well, you'll have to try to remember what was said in your report then. Tell me what it was like. Were you pleased with it?'

'No, Miss,' said Darren, then warming to his task, he added, 'Well, bits of it were all right.'

'Yes?' interjected Kate hopefully. 'Which bits?'

'The PE and that,' said Darren.

This is getting us nowhere, thought Kate. Instructing the luckless Darren to wait, even though he had not had his 'break', Kate went off to get herself a copy of the report from the file.

'Right,' she said on her return. 'Now we can see a bit more clearly why I wanted to see you. What parts of your school life have you got to improve on – according to this?'

'Well, I'm a little behind on coursework,' came the tentative reply.

They talked about this problem, and discussed strategies to help Darren catch up.

'What does this mean?' asked Kate. '"Darren must apply himself more conscientiously to this subject. He needs to understand that he will not achieve his potential unless he behaves in a more mature manner in class and begins to take his studies seriously".'

'Oh, yes, well, that's because I can't do it, and Miss thinks I should be able to,' he said, sounding aggrieved. D1

'It seems to me that "Miss" thinks you should do everybody a favour and behave yourself in her lessons in a proper manner. What do you think? Is she right to complain about you? What do you do that's wrong?'

'Talking and that. Miss Whigley sent me out yesterday. She said I called out across the room, but I never.'

'Well, you surprise me. You seem such a pleasant, sensible person here in my room. D2 I would have thought you'd have the sense to realise that you need good GCSEs in order to get on in life - this subject is so important these days!'

'Yes, but I'm no good at it. But I'm going to be better now. I'm going to get all up to date and try a bit harder.' D3

'Why have you decided that now, when you could have made that decision ages ago?'

'Well, it's not worth it, is it? All this!'

'Do you mean the hassle of coming to see me?'

'Yes, missing my break an' that. You'll see, Miss, I'm going to be good from now on.'

Kate sent Darren off with the promise that she would be following up his progress and she expected to hear better reports of him soon, particularly from Miss Whigley. D4 How many Darrens were there? Kate thought back through the term's in-service work. Does the department have adequate support to deal with the Darrens of this world, and more importantly, does it think it has that support? The department had met regularly and discussed many different aspects of their teaching – had these sessions been of any practical help? Had they helped anyone to teach Darren to learn? She wondered what they thought about the situation. She went down to talk to Miss Whigley.

'Ah, hello, Sue! How're things going?'

'Fine, thank you!' replied Sue.

'Children behaving themselves?'

'Yes, more or less. By the way, I was going to see you. I lost half my tooth at the weekend, and the only time the dentist can fit me in is tomorrow. Is it all right if I go then? It's period five and it's my non-contact time.'

'Yes, that sounds OK – just jot it down on a piece of paper and put it in my tray so I don't forget! By the way, I saw Darren this morning about his report. I told him I'd be keeping an eye on his general progress, and particularly on these lessons.'

'OK, I'll keep you informed.'

'How is he these days?'

'Oh, so so. Could be better.'

'Would you like to come and talk to me about him?'   D5

Sue came and talked. She found Darren's behaviour difficult to control. He called out, interrupted, forgot his books, didn't do his homework, said he couldn't understand her, just generally didn't seem to try, didn't want to try.   D6

Using the story in an INSET session

At the next inservice session I gave the story to the teachers to read. I did not say that it was based on my experiences as I was hoping to focus more on the department, on what the teachers thought about the situation in the story and whether they could relate it to their own experiences. I felt satisfied that each member of the department could cope with reading and discussing the story without embarrassment or distress, although one of them did remark: 'I think I must have written more or less that comment on about half of my students' reports!'

We divided into two groups initially to discuss the story, and then returned for a departmental discussion. The session was animated and everybody participated. With the agreement of the group I taped the group discussion in which I participated and the main discussion. I finished the session by saying, 'One of the things you might find useful is to write your own story in response. This might help to expose some of the things you are thinking are happening to you, and how you feel about the support you're getting ...'

The next inservice session took place four weeks later. I had used my notes to sum up the main points raised by the discussion in the form of 19 statements. I did this because I did not wish to identify what each person had said. My idea was to give teachers the opportunity to think about which of the statements was an issue for them. I had produced a set of empty booklets entitled *Reflecting on my Classroom Experiences*. I had made six copies of each of the statements, printed them onto card, and arranged them in piles. I asked each member of the department to take whichever cards they thought was 'true for me at the moment', and to stick them in their booklet. Below are the 19 statements ranked in order of how many teachers selected them as pertinent to their current situation.

❏ I find it helpful when we exchange practical ideas about methodology (6).

❏ The pupils need to understand that they have to put effort into learning the subject (5).

❏ I think it's important to build up a good relationship in the classroom (5).

❏ I find that Year 8 pupils are very positive about their subject lessons (4).

❏ I would like someone to come into my room to give me advice on my teaching style (3).

❏ I accept my responsibility for the 'Darrens' in my classroom, but I need someone to tell me what strategies they have tried out and found to work with their 'Darrens' (3).

❏ I am confident that I differentiate the work reasonably well, but I am still trying to find better ways to do this (3).

❏ I would like easier access to the departmental store of resources/ worksheets (3).

❏ I come up against the view 'what's the point of learning this subject?' (3).

❏ I find that I struggle to get the interest of Year 9 (3).

❏ I find it very helpful to use my non-contact time to sit with another member of the department and talk about my teaching experiences (2).

❏ I am not sure about how to differentiate the work, and still manage the class adequately (2).

❏ The curriculum for Year 9 is not so interesting (2).

❏ Managing homework – how do I cope if only three of the class do their homework? They offer many different excuses – it's hard to deal fairly with all of them if there are such a lot (2).

❏ The curriculum for Year 8 is lively and relevant (1).

❏ I feel frustrated when I cannot carry on from the last lesson because children have 'forgotten' their books (1).

❏ I find it hard to move Year 9 on from where they were in Year 8. For instance, they see some parts of the curriculum as having been covered already last year (0).

❏ One child can ruin the relationship I've built up (0).

❏ I think other people should deal with 'Darren' (0).

All six members chose 'I find it helpful when we exchange practical ideas about methodology'. I would take from this the clear message that this form of inservice is thought to be particularly useful, and therefore should happen often. Five out of six teachers thought that pupils needed to understand that they had to put effort into learning the subject, and three teachers chose the item suggesting that pupils did not see the point of learning the subject. Five teachers chose the item about the importance of building up a good relationship in the classroom. Four out of six found that Year 8 pupils were very positive about their lessons, while three admitted that it was a struggle to get the interest of year 9. There was some interest in the relative merit of the curriculum for both years with two teachers saying that the year 9 curriculum was not interesting and one saying that the year 8 curriculum was lively and relevant. Three of the items that received three nominations suggested areas where the teachers would have liked further support. The rest of the items received two or fewer nominations, and three items were not chosen by any of the teachers.

I had constructed the story of 'Darren' from my own experiences, events and dilemmas, and this had made sense to me. I wanted to know how department A experienced their world, so I gave them the story to think about and comment upon because the mind is constantly engaged in the process of building models, and in creating the world according to its own mix of cultural and individual expectations (Chafe, 1990:81; Carter, 1993:7).

I was expecting and therefore not surprised to find that the dilemmas brought out by the department were different from the ones I had felt when writing the story. My colleagues' dilemmas can be seen from the main points I summarised of the discussion and by linking some of the statements. They were:

1. I think it's important to build up a good relationship in the classroom, but one child can ruin the relationship I've built up. (Statements 1 and 18)

2. The curriculum for year 8 is lively and relevant, and year 8 pupils are very positive about their lessons, but the curriculum in year 9 is not so interesting, and I struggle to keep the pupils' interest. I think they see some parts of the curriculum as having been covered before. (Statements 15, 4 as opposed to 10, 13 and 17)

3. I think I know about differentiating the work, but am still trying to find better ways of doing this and of managing the class adequately whilst I am doing it. (Statements 7 and 12)

4. I find it very helpful when we exchange practical ideas about methodology, and often use my non-contact time to talk to other

colleagues about my teaching, but I would like someone to come into my room to give me advice on my teaching style, and on strategies for dealing with the Darrens of this world. (Statements 1, 11 and 5,6)

This analysis suggested that most of my dilemmas had not been replicated by the department, and that I had not had uppermost in my mind the ones they had emphasised. We had shared some dilemmas: I was concerned about the pupils' behaviour and what we needed to do to improve it, and the department was similarly concerned. They had practical solutions to offer: exchanging ideas, talking to other colleagues, having someone else in the classroom to observe and advise, and seeking advice on how best to deal with 'Darren'.

The story had given the teachers in Department A the opportunity to raise issues about classroom practice, and the session that followed had enabled them to prioritise some of the issues that they had raised and consider which of them were most important. They had also been able to share in each other's prioritising, with the possible consequence of understanding each other's needs better. I had been able to establish some of the perspectives we shared and also I had some useful feedback about the way in which I had managed staff development activities.

Encouraging teachers to write their own stories

Not long after these INSET sessions, Martin approached me and asked if I would like to read the story he had written. We called it 'Untitled'. I have Martin's permission to use it.

The Story 'Untitled'

As he looked at the cover board, immediate panic! His HOD was absent and he hadn't had any news from her. There were 5 minutes until the bell and the PGCE student was going to be teaching her first lesson, so it was important that he, the second in the department, was there at the beginning of the lesson. First things first – ring the HOD for some cover work.

He made his way back to the department office.

'Harriet's just phoned,' said one of the other teachers. 'Here's her work. Would you like me to write it out for you?'

'Oh, thanks. That would be really useful.' Was the panic that obvious in his face? 'Put it on my desk and I'll start the lesson off.'

He knew that this was not ideal, and certainly not the sort of beginning he had hoped to give the PGCE student, but there really was nothing else to do. He went into the HOD's lesson and started

---

to explain the work. The cover teacher was late. Another panic! Ten minutes into the lesson. He couldn't leave the children. What was the PGCE student doing? There was shouting coming from one of the other classrooms. What should come first? His panic was momentarily relieved when one of the Deputy Headteachers appeared in the corridor.

'Shall I stay here ...' said the Deputy Head. She didn't need to finish the sentence!

He returned to his teaching room to watch the student. At least he now had a few minutes to sort himself out. For lesson 3 he had agreed to go and watch Alistair, one of the other teachers in the department. He'd done that the previous week and had a really fruitful 'feed-back' session.

Now it was going to be the case of would the other teacher put the agreed suggestions into practice? He made himself 'switch-into' what was happening in the lesson now. It was going well, very well; this student was going to be good to work with. At least that was one good thing to look forward to in the next few weeks. The rest of the morning – up to break – went very quickly.

As the bell went for the end of break, he had high hopes that the lesson he was going to observe would show progress. The teacher was already at the classroom door making sure the children entered the room in a relatively orderly fashion and that they hung their coats up. Even though to others this might have seemed such a small step, it was really good to see. To know that he could support others and that his advice was valued and acted upon had long been an issue of great concern to the extent that he was beginning to wonder what his own strengths really were. As the lesson went on, he became more uplifted. The behaviour of the group was much improved. Most of them were listening and participating and Alistair was being more assertive. There was still a long way to go but at least everyone should have been feeling that progress could be made if everyone was prepared to work at it and really want it to happen.

He left the room at the end of lesson 3 to return to his 6th form group. Barely had he sat down when there was a knock at the door. There stood one of the newer members of the department.

'Could you take these two? They just won't shut up.'

He wanted to say 'No', he wanted to say, 'What have you done about the talking?' but didn't feel he could interrupt his own lesson any more. There was also the fact that somewhere down the corridor was another group without a teacher. So he said 'Yes!'

> He went to switch on the video to continue his 6th form lesson. Another knock at the door.
>
> 'Sir says can you come to the room please?'
>
> What could be wrong? He left his group to see what the problem was.
>
> 'They are awful. They won't listen, won't sit down; just look at the floor! They are throwing things about!'
>
> There wasn't time to wonder what had gone wrong. Yet again he found himself in a situation where he couldn't act as he wanted to.
>
> He proceeded to tell the class how pleased he had been earlier and how disappointed he now felt that some of them had let the group down. He set them a target – hopefully an achievable one – to do by the end of the lesson. The familiar feeling of frustration reappeared. Would progress ever be made? He seemed to be wasting all his efforts.
>
> He returned to his 6th form room, sat down and tried to concentrate on the video. The classroom door opened. 'You couldn't come and talk to my group ...?'

Martin came to see me to discuss *'Untitled'* soon after he had given me the story. We talked about his frustration that things were not getting better swiftly enough for his liking. We talked about the support he needed, and about whether what he was doing with and for individuals was helpful for the department. At the end of the meeting we agreed a number of strategies. Martin would make a video of one of his lessons so we could use it as a basis for inservice work. He would also talk to Alistair about making a video of one of Alistair's lessons, to help Alistair see what was happening in the classroom, how he tended to retreat from being assertive, and let the pupils 'take control' of the situation.

Martin's story was a fictionalised account but there were autobiographical elements and he was concerned about whether he should have written it, in much the same way as I worried about *The Canterbury Tales*. What would the 'participants' think if they read it? He was not researching his practice in quite the same way as I was, in that he was not consciously trying to practise action research and so he did not have to meet the ethical imperative of empowering others, towards which I was striving. He used the story as a form of self-exploration, and as a result was able to move his practice forward. Although it took Martin some time to organise the video, he eventually did so, and he and I watched the tape of his lesson. We followed this up by showing it to the rest of the department in the inservice session.

I had constructed 'Martin' in *The Canterbury Tales* and I was struck by some points of similarity with the Martin projected by himself. Both stories showed Martin as in a position of trying to help his colleagues, and being prepared to do so; of being concerned with order and children's learning; and of knowing the need for Alistair to be more assertive with his classes. Interestingly, both stories showed Martin's frustration with the teachers he was helping, but in the story *'Untitled'* and also in the discussion afterwards, the frustration came across much more strongly than it had in my story.

There was no criticism in Martin's story of other members of his department, whereas in my construction of Martin, there had been. This did not mean necessarily that Martin had not been critical, merely that he had not chosen to express it in his story. I think Martin's own story indicated a greater degree of care on his part than I had built into him in my story, and this led me to revise my view of him as a result.

I was pleased I had been able to give back to the department a story which was relevant, yet accessible for them, and from which one of them was able to write his own story. Reverting to the purposes of writing a story of our educational experiences, the key ones in this context were for reflexivity on the part of the writer, opportunities to open the way for different interpretations to take place, self-exploration for the readers, and dialectical critique, searching out dilemmas and contradictions, and the readers' engagement of their own experiences with those of the story. Connelly and Clandinin (1990, p.124) said, 'Looking at life as narrative or storied allows us to see the unities, continuities and discontinuities, images and rhythms in our lives. We take the view that one of the basic human forms of experiences of the world is a story and that the storied quality of experiences is both unconsciously restoried in life and consciously storied, retold and relived through processes of reflection'. This seems a powerful tool to use in promoting both our own and other's education!

Chapter 9

Working in partnership to implement teacher research

Pamela Lomax and Moyra Evans

> [Tape 1:1] One of the reasons I wanted to join this group was because I wanted to look at my practice. I didn't think I was relating smoothly with colleagues and certainly the frustrations that I felt in the classroom were quite frankly oppressing me. I realised that the results I wanted for children to achieve and for me to achieve just were not happening and I began to really worry about my practice.

The writer is one of a group of teachers from a Secondary School where I, Moyra, am deputy headteacher with responsibility for staff development. Over the last four years I have been registered for a Ph.D. which has focused on implementing staff development in which teachers use an action research methodology, selecting their own area of focus, using experiential learning and working in collaboration with colleagues to develop reflective practice. I, Pam, have been instrumental in negotiating the procedures through which the teachers' school-based work can be accredited by the university for a post graduate qualification and I have also worked with Moyra as director of study for her Ph.D. We do not want to dwell on the success of the model of staff development implied by this work because it has been validated in a number of ways:

❐ it was recognised through the partnership awards made by the RSA in 1994 as a worthy experiment in partnership between a school and higher education

❐ it was confirmed by the success of teachers in attaining post graduate qualifications from the university in 1994 and 1995 as a worthy route through which teachers' school based work is accredited

❐ it has been recognised through the refereeing process, and through citation and publication in the educational press as a high quality contribution to an aspect of educational management (Lomax and Evans, 1995; 1996; Evans, 1995a; Pimenoff, 1995)

We have chosen two episodes as the practical focus from which we attempt to make critical certain aspects of our partnership that are potentially problematic to us (Tripp, 1993). We intend, through an analysis of this specific data, to evaluate our own motives and actions as teacher educators in relation to the distinctly *educational* values that we see as underpinning our work. From this we hope to draw conclusions about the contribution that a co-researcher self-study action research approach can make to an educational epistemology of practice.

Memory work as self-study

Action research includes a strong tradition of critical reflection on one's own values and actions, and in this sense self-study is an integral aspect of it. We wanted to explore, in more depth than usual, the educative relationship that made possible our partnership. To do this we decided to use a method called *memory work*. Memory work is particularly apt for self-study as it is only possible if the object and subject of the research are the same, where the object of the research becomes the researcher. Memory work is a method for a collective investigation of experience, where each member of a group can draw upon her own experience in order to help another understand hers better.

The seminal work on memory work can be found in a paper by Frigga Haug and others (1987) about *Female Sexuality* and has been used by women such as June Crawford (1992) and her colleagues who explored *Emotion and Gender*. More recently Michael Schratz (1994) has written about the use of memory work as collective self-reflection within an action research perspective. Haug and Crawford emphasise the importance of working towards a group understanding of a shared concern resulting in a contribution to knowledge. In this way they conceived memory work as active and interventionist leading to possible social reconstruction rather than an airing of merely personal feelings and interpretations.

The method of memory work is often based on the use of story. Individuals write stories about some aspect of their life and present these stories to a group to discuss, not as a representation of the self but just as a story. By drawing upon the others' experiences of similar events the author can clarify her own active part in the events she has described and place them in a broader social and political setting. As a result of the discussions, the author goes away and rewrites the story, not necessarily to change her fundamental beliefs about things that are expressed in the story, but perhaps to give a different emphasis on some aspect of it that has emerged through the discussion. Often the stories are written in the third person, with the author being represented by a fictional character, thus enabling her to stand back from her own experience. The stories focus on the historical 'I' that has created the meaning so that it can become the subject of an interrogation by the group. It is not just the words of the story, but the gaps and spaces in the account, the things written between the lines, that are explored.

Haug's work is particularly interesting because it is based on a well articulated ontological position. She rejects views of socialisation which 'coyly circumvent the active participation of individuals in their formation as social beings' (p.33) in favour of seeing people as active participants, playing a part in creating the structures that confine them. Memory work is a means of deconstructing past experience so that we can take control of what we choose to be.

An adaptation of memory work

For our own self-study we, Moyra and Pam, have adapted the method of memory work described above. We will focus on our work together creating a school-university partnership to support teacher in-service development. Many accounts about this work exist in archived data about the partnership: in written records and tape recorded conversations. They were not produced specifically for self-study purposes, but they could be seen to represent the stories we have told to each other and the plays we have created and recorded about our work.

We chose to focus on two texts which are transcripts of conversations that took place during the course of our partnership. We dealt with both transcripts in an 8 hour session that took place in February 1995, 9 months and 2 years respectively after the taped meetings had taken place. The procedure that we adopted was that we each focused on one of the texts which we carefully read, highlighting words, sentences and passages that we thought were significant. We then took turns to help each other explore the chosen texts, extrapolating new meanings and reading between the lines. We recognised the difference between what we intended to do as a group of two whose stimulus was to be texts of conversations recorded in the past and what Haug and others had done, which was to write stories specifically for a group to discuss with a definite intention in mind in writing the story. We were aware of the importance of other people in the circle and conscious that we would miss their different perspectives. However, we relied on the fact that in the intervening period between the original discussion from which our text was created, and the present, both of us had changed and could bring a fresh perspective to the old issues. We also thought that we could treat our voices in the transcript as if they were the voices of other people, as to some extent the transcript itself objectified our earlier conversations. In this way we were able to stand apart from ourselves in order to see the praxis emerge more clearly. We taped our conversations so that we could use the records as a basis for us each to write a further story. These stories represent the outcome of our memory work, the form of the story itself being the vehicle through which we have chosen to represent our study.

Setting scene one

It was a meeting in which Moyra, Pam and six teachers from the School had presented their work to two people from Industry who were acting as assessors for a prize for innovative partnerships in open learning. The transcript is mainly of the teachers' voices as they talk about their own action research.

Pam highlighted parts of the transcript that seemed significant to her. She underlined words and metaphors that she liked and also passages where she thought the teachers' work reflected her own educational values. Moyra used the highlighted passages as a prompt *to help Pam explore* the connection between what teachers said and the *invisible part* that Pam had played in their research. This method of jointly reflecting on a shared experience enabled both Pam and Moyra to reach new understandings about their partnership.

Pam's story

> [Teacher: Tape 9.48] We talk at great length about what it is about these meetings that means we stay there till six o'clock, six-thirty, without worrying and having to rush off home ... whereas with other meetings, by the time you get to five o'clock you are looking at your watch thinking, 'I'm going to go.' The meetings are so engaging. Why is this? What is it about this group? ... and it isn't the people because we probably work more closely on a day to day basis with other people or with our tutor teams or whatever. It is the nature of the work, because the work is so personal to us, so important to us as

individuals ... I always go away from here feeling so much better ... the stresses and worries and the tiredness have gone. I feel fired up again to start teaching. [Tape 1.1] ... from the first meeting I realised that it was going to be unlike any learning that I had experienced, it was going to allow me to focus on an area that I thought was going to be important and to be able to use my own classroom practice ... it's this bringing to the fore my own agenda. [Tape 2.8] and it's just been amazing the way I think I have enjoyed and experienced and in some ways refined and improved this phenomenon which is action research ... that's just been amazing, it's encouraged a form of quality of learning, a quality of ownership, an engagement ...

Pam: all the words I underlined were words about action research as distinct from other kinds of research. They demonstrate really well the exciting thing about practitioner research where you have ownership of your own work ... where you can make your own choices ... the words describe active participation in one's own learning ... and that is one of the aims I would have in most of my teaching ... to make my students active learners ... there are also teachers' statements about what their pupils have achieved as a result of their action research, for example the teacher who talks about the way in which her action research 'cascades down into the classroom' and the teacher who describes how she felt she 'was walking on air' after a child had shown his appreciation of the lesson. It is the knowledge that there is a possible link between me in the university, through to Moyra in the school, to the teachers implementing it in their classroom and the children being excited ... that makes me want to explore the process further.

Pam sees the action research of the teachers as a celebration of her own values about learning and research. She can connect to their work through Moyra. Moyra questions this position and points to the hierarchical relation of Pam and the teachers. Pam sees a correspondence between her position and that of Moyra because Moyra must look to evidence of improvement in pupils' work to judge her success in working with the teachers, as Pam must look to improvement in teachers' work to judge her success in working with Moyra. The fact that the teachers express Pam's values so clearly seems to her to validate her educative work with Moyra.

[Teacher: Tape 4.24] I've tried out various things with various classes and I've always been very out front with them ... and one day one student at the end of the lesson ... he came up and said ... 'I just wanted to say something, that it's the best lesson we've ever had' ... and I felt I was walking on air ... this child had said this, and that was a direct result of what we had been doing ... and yes I think the students do notice, because there is a huge difference in me now and I am a different person and they can't fail to miss that ...

Pam: the fact that a teacher can claim to be a different person and that her pupils 'cannot fail to miss that' is evidence for me of the transformational potential of teacher action research. I believe that we are capable of affecting things and making changes for the better ... and a lot of people don't seem to think that ... they seem to believe that one's life history controls the possibilities of what they can do.

How does Pam interact with Moyra to enable Moyra to interact with teachers? Is Moyra's part in the relationship simply that of a student who has been active in constructing her story for Pam, her teacher, to critique? It has been on the basis of this joint learning and research that Pam and Moyra have, together, been able to set up this action research partnership between the school and the university, and been able to persuade their separate organisations that this is a mutually beneficial thing to do.

Pam: I don't see it as a one-way relationship. My values and practice have been clarified and transformed as the educative relationship with Moyra has developed. Moyra has played an active part in creating this relationship and has recreated and transformed it (not reproduced it) in her relationship with the teachers. I also see myself reflected back when I read Moyra's writing, some of which has been based on transcripts of taped conversations between us ... and when I respond to Moyra's writing, by writing in the margins of her papers, I am taking an active part in Moyra's construction of meaning from our relationship.

[Teacher: Tape 8.42] ... that's been so integral in my write up, my use of the story, and I might add very pleasing as well ... but the nature of this learning is so very different and it's more active ... and I've been involved with courses beforehand, part time courses where one's received packages of material and one's attended tutorials and one's had all manner of support from fellow students ... but I have never been able to site the agenda, perhaps utilize experience ... in the way that I have been able to do on this particular course.

The writing of Frigga Haug (1987) suggested to us the division of labour between writers and authors, between writing and literature. Moyra is worried that the teachers do not get on with 'writing up the account' although she has seen that they have done the action research and can defend their claims to have improved their practices. Pam is concerned that the external examiners will find the teachers' reports unacceptable because they are not embedded in the traditional literature reviews. But Moyra has seen teachers' stories and heard them read from their diaries; and the teachers' reports that Pam has read communicate directly, as one 'I' to another, the authentic lived experience of having been part of a process of educational change. Should we demand more than this? Do we not ourselves, Moyra and Pam, use writing as 'a transgression of boundaries, an exploration of new territories' and so 'become involved in the destruction of culture' that Haug describes so well? What kind of writing do we demand that disables highly literate people from explaining in written words the work they have done?

> [Teacher: Tape 10.49] For a long time I was a little perplexed because I thought this can't be really educational because it seems to be so me-centred ... forgive me but this was my process of growing! I then began to think, well no, it's trying to use everything that is happening to me in my professional experience and understand it ... it was all right to be doing something with a colleague ... and it was all right to be using some concerns and showing how I unknotted the problem of what was going to be my focus through a narrative ... it was just lovely really.

As action researchers we are me-centred when we take measures to live out our educational values. Whitehead (1993:67-77) says that as 'living contradictions' we must constantly strive to resolve an unresolvable state if we are to improve our practice as educators. To do this we must be able to stand back from ourselves and see ourselves as others see us. But we do not find it easy 'to look into our own eyes' or 'to understand our own understanding'. Moyra uses writing to help her stand back from her own understanding. She uses 'fictional' writing to bring together her experiences and her feelings and her thoughts about what is happening. By putting them into a story she is able to understand better the experiences that she has already been through and thought about, in ways that she would not have dreamed other than through writing. Pam uses academic writing for the same purpose, as a way of distancing herself from her experience so that she can see it more clearly. She makes this writing public to get different challenges to her thoughts from a lot of different perspectives. But is such writing an acceptable representation of Pam's self-study? Should the personal and private 'I' speak more directly as the teachers' 'I' and Moyra's 'I' speak in their stories. Why should their fictional 'I' be more authentic than the 'I' that is author of the academic paper and can claim its words, its thoughts and its values as true representations of an intended meaning in a chosen form?

Setting scene two

Moyra had confided in Pam, her tutor, her concerns about the ethical questions that were arising in her action research at the school. Pam was particularly interested in action research and ethics at that time and the meeting was partly to consider whether they could write a joint paper about ethical issues in action research. Moyra had made the transcript of the meeting for that purpose, although they had never written the paper. Now, two years later Moyra read the transcript carefully and highlighted the parts that seemed significant to her. Like Pam, with the previous text, she underlined words and metaphors that she liked and also passages that suggested dilemmas. Pam used the highlighted passages as a prompt *to help Moyra explore* issues to do with what Moyra has termed hierarchical relations.

Moyra's story

'I've just been talking to Pam about that discussion she and I had two years ago to the day, February 23, 1993!' said Self 95, in a musing kind of way.

Self 93 sharpened up her defences.

'Oh?' she said, and the guardedness was there in her voice. Self 95 heard it clearly, but couldn't pull away from what she'd started.

'We read through the transcript of the tape. Do you remember what it was all about?' she asked.

'Yes,' replied Self 93 defensively. 'It was all about my action research and teachers in school, and Harriet and ethics – my ethics in writing a story about Harriet, who was one of the teachers, and then not giving it to her so she could see what I'd written.'

'Yes, and if you remember,' gloated Self 95, 'Pam told you at the time that you should have given the story to Harriet. But you never did, did you?'

'No, I didn't,' replied Self 93, 'and I'm very pleased. I'm still convinced that Harriet couldn't have coped with it.'

'Ah, that's all very well, but you never gave her the chance of showing you, did you? You thought you knew best. Don't you see it differently now?' asked Self 95 sweetly.

93 was not to be tripped up so easily. She put an obstacle in the way so that 95 would have to slow down.

'Why are you asking?' she enquired. 'What were you talking to Pam about that for anyway?' She sounded as though 95 didn't have the right to resuscitate the debate.

'Well,' replied 95, importantly, 'Pam and I are engaging in some self-study for the AERA conference. I hope to meet all these people whose works I keep reading. The ones who are interested in stories, and selves and so on.'

93 was pleased to have diverted 95 from probing deeper for a moment or two. But 95 was tenacious.

'Getting back to that discussion – I'm not sure that it was all about ethics now. We went through the transcript yesterday, and highlighted some of the issues we thought were important. It's strange, but we got into quite an emotionally charged debate! All about you, 93! I was pleased it wasn't about me!'

95 realised as she said this that it wasn't really true. But for the purposes of the discussion now with 93, it would do. 95 suspected that the argument with Pam was all to do with her, 95, but she wasn't going to face that yet. Let's tease 93 some more, she thought.

'Yes, why didn't you face up to your Headteacher?' she asked. She had always wanted to know the answer to this one – she was on tenterhooks – would she find out now?

93 went pale.

'Yes, you see,' continued 95 relentlessly, 'Pam said that discussion was all about you – she said it's about 93 and her relationship with the Head, 93 and her relationship with Harriet, 93 and the ethics of all this, and 93 trying to look objectively at herself.'

95 stopped to see how this was going down. Then she said, 'Actually I felt quite sorry for you – I did defend you, honestly!'

Of course, what had happened was that 95 had been under the spotlight, not 93 at all. 95 hadn't liked it, so was looking around for someone to blame, so that she could feel better.

Pam had started it all off when she picked on something that 95 had said when she was 93 – 'No, but the Head tends to be right an awful lot of the time', and Pam had disagreed with this. She didn't think the Head was right all the time, and implied that 93 should have known that. 95 felt guilty because she recognised that she should have challenged the Head more than she did – both as 93 and 95, but hadn't. She didn't want to know why not. She knew why not and she didn't want to talk about it. She didn't want Pam to know. And certainly she didn't want the rest of the world to know. Actually, the person she didn't want to know more than anybody else, was the Head.

So she'd said to Pam, 'This self-study is all very well, but if a self doesn't want to face herself, I think she should have the right not to.'

'Yes, I agree,' said Pam, in a very obliging and totally surprising sort of way, such that 95 was caught off guard. 'We can say, I don't want to take this any further at this time. Maybe it is a dangerous thing to do this exposing and we're not ready for it yet.'

95 and Pam had continued their discussion, but none of it was quite so morbidly fascinating as that part.

Moyra listened to the tape of their discussion as she drove home. She tossed and turned in the night trying to make sense of her thoughts. She wrote notes of the tapes. There were two major things troubling her: first, why did she feel so bad about the discussion with Pam about the Head; and second, how was she going to and indeed, could she, record any self-study?

Self 95-1 debated with self 95-2.

95-1 said to 95-2, 'This business of relationships – it calls into question all my relationships with people who project themselves as authoritative people – who know what they think, and who know that they know. I cannot penetrate their thinking. If I argue with them, they always know what to say in reply. They aren't ever offput whilst they think of the answer. Therefore, I think **they** know, and **I** don't. I see this as a weakness in me that I don't want other people to see.'

95-2 replied, 'Is what you mean that you think you are being controlled by people who know? You don't like being controlled, but are at a loss to know how to exert yourself to change the relationship, and you don't want to talk about it because you perceive it to be a weakness?'

95-1 laughed and said, 'Yes, that's about right. And why should the rest of the world need to know this?'

95-2 replied, 'Perhaps because unless you are encouraged into a situation in which you have to confront yourself, you may not do it. Perhaps self-study needs to be social from that point of view, in the same way as your action research principles are strongly social, aren't they?'.

95 went back to talk to 93. She wanted answers to questions now – she'd quit playing with 93's feelings.

'Why did you try to protect Harriet from seeing her inadequacies?' Self 95 asked Self 93.

'I was protecting her,' replied 93, 'because I thought it would be unkind of me to put her under any more pressure at the time. She wouldn't have been able to cope with it, and it would have been counterproductive.'

'But did you feel that she couldn't speak up for herself? That she couldn't hold herself accountable for her actions?'

'No, that's not what it was about,' replied 93. 'It's got to do with **me** and how I would have felt about highlighting her inadequacy in this particular way at this particular time. I felt I had a responsibility to protect vulnerable people and try to bring about change in them, but in less confrontational ways.'

'Like as a parent might protect her child?' asked 95.

'Just so, like as a parent,' reaffirmed 93.

'How would you feel if someone did that to you?' asked 95.

'I suppose I'd feel aggrieved that I wasn't being treated like an equal – if I knew about it. But I wouldn't want to argue about it. I'd try to work my way around it, peaceably, but ultimately, if I couldn't, I'd resign myself to a quiet life.'

An uneasy quiet fell between them.

95 broke it with, 'Looking back at the conversation – just two years ago exactly, there seems to have been a lot of paternalism about!'

'Yes, I think I could be accused of being paternalistic in looking after Harriet, and my perceptions of the Head were that she was acting as an all-powerful parent towards me – but I don't know that I saw that at the time. What about Pam – where does she fit in all this study of myself?' asked 93.

'I think she sees the study of herself in how well the teachers at our school have taken to the action research process,' replied 95. 'I am looking forward to reading her account. I wonder whether she might see a bit of paternalism there?

Self 95 had tapes and transcripts and notes and papers all around her. She was deeply into worrying about what her old self might be saying to her new self about the ethics of protecting Harriet, when suddenly she saw a way of conveying her thought about herself incorporating her own work on writing stories. She believed she could show an aspect of the study of herself through a story – she knew she could detach herself from the pain of the self knowledge if she were to write about someone else. Self 93 was the obvious choice. She set to work with enthusiasm.

'I've just been talking to Pam about that discussion she and I had two years ago to the day, February 25, 1993!' she said to Self 93, in a musing kind of way.......

Concluding reflections

Our aim in writing this paper about our partnership was to evaluate our own motives and actions as teacher educators in relation to the educational values that we have espoused. Our two stories represent the outcome of our memory work. We have used a different form to represent this from the usual written record, one that is more in line with new ideas about representing research (Cole and Knowles, 1994; Lomax and Parker 1995; MacLure, 1993). The stories incorporate our new description and explanation of an aspect of our partnership and demonstrate the educative relationship of Pam and Moyra, as the basis upon which the partnership in teacher education was possible. What has become clear to us, is that these stories are only a beginning to other memory work. We intend to meet together and challenge each other further on what we have written and redraft our stories in line with the original method devised by Haug and her colleagues. We will also be able to incorporate into this future work the responses we get from you, the readers of this account, if you will feed back your observations to us.

Much of our work has been within the institutional contexts within which we spend much of our time (school and university) and this chapter has not addressed the political side of implementing successful innovation. Even so we hope that our work provides some evidence to counteract those grim analyses that suggest that in the UK the technical goals of schools and the bureaucratic goals of Universities always outweigh their educational goals. The circle of events is all important: the university tutor supports the school based tutor; the school based tutor supports the teachers; the teachers' practice changes and pupils benefit; and the theory that teachers are able to extrapolate from the process informs the knowledge base of Education. We hope that our work may suggest a model whereby both school and university can work in partnership to promote education and thus prevent the divide predicted by Cochran-Smith and Lytle in their commentary on teacher research (1990).

Our partnership between institutions has led to educational developments for both. The school has benefited from the structure and support which the university has provided, and can claim to be amongst the first providers of an accredited teacher education programme. Teacher research provides new knowledge about the processes and products of teaching. In their case studies the teachers demonstrate a movement from the technical rationality model of professional knowledge to the continuously growing model of the reflective practitioner (Schön, 1983). The action research has stimulated questions which have no easy answers and has provided the learning climate through which the teachers have shifted their situated frames of knowledge (Evans, 1993). It has broken the 'default settings' of their daily lives in classrooms (Barnes, 1992) and enabled them to reach out for new understandings. It is the latter that enables us to draw conclusions in line with our second aim, about the significance of a co-researcher self-study action research approach to the emergence of a distinctively educational (as opposed to social science) form of research. We believe that the form we have used for theorising our work suggests new ways of representing qualitative work that will support some of the arguments being presented in recent issues of *Educational Researcher* (Delandshere and Petrosky, 1994; Eisner, 1993; Moss, 1994; Richardson, 1994) and in innovative case studies such as Cole and Knowles (1994); Convery (1993); Ghaye and Wakefield (1993); MacLure (1993); Russell and Munby (1992); Schratz (1993b). We believe that teachers' case studies provide the ammunition with which university schools of Education can claim their own distinctly educational knowledge base that need no longer rely on that of social science.

Chapter 10

How can we help educational managers establish and implement effective 'critical' friendships?

Pamela Lomax, Cathie Woodward and Zoe Parker

This paper is written from the perspective of tutors in higher education who facilitate educational managers' action research. I, Pam, am course director of an MA: School and College Management programme, and I, Cathie, and I, Zoe, have been tutors on the programme. We have all at one time or other engaged in learning relationships with each other and Zoe and Cathie have formally sought each other out as critical friends. The educational managers who are students on the programme are drawn from diverse parts of the education system, and are engaged in action research towards a final dissertation. As part of the programme, they are expected to establish a working relationship with a work colleague who will provide supportive but 'critical' friendship during the period of the research, and will take part in a meeting set up in the university to validate the research. Recently, an external examiner has questioned the course model of critical friend as one which could result in 'collusion' rather than 'critique', and he has expressed concern about the efficacy of involving work colleagues in the validation of action research. This paper examines these criticisms in the context of a wider exploration of the role of the critical friend in action research. It concludes that the criticisms are based on a mis-informed view of the purpose of critical friends within the course model; nor are they supported by teachers' accounts of their own research or other course evaluation data. The paper concludes by identifying the main dimensions of the critical friendship role and suggests ways in which this might be developed into a 'learning relationship' that is particularly congruent with the model of action research we promote.

Action research and the masters programme

We see action research as a disciplined method for improving practices in order to bring about educationally worthwhile outcomes. The action researcher needs to describe and explain the values that underpin her educational practices, make a disciplined and critical study of these practices, and work towards a solution to the dilemmas that have been identified. We believe that co-operation and collaboration are essential to this because *learning relationships* are at the heart of educational activity, and improvement implies making changes that involve others (Lomax, 1991b:2-7). For these reasons participants are expected to conduct their action research within a set of principles which include the imperative of trying to make their action research participatory (Lomax, 1991b:103-105). The principle of participation means that:

❐ action researchers must be participants in the action, not outside researchers observing the action;
❐ they must work to involve colleagues who are part of the action, in the research process;
❐ they should be tolerant of others who must learn from experience; and
❐ they should aim for collective action and collaboration.

Collaborative intent on the part of the action researcher is an incentive to ask colleagues to give critical feedback about one's own practice, encourage them to share the educational experience of being an action researcher, persuade them to become co-researchers, and be prepared to relinquish ownership of action when colleagues are ready to take it over. Participants are advised to be open, as the integrity of action research depends on avoiding manipulating others. They need to be ready to take risks and possibly expose others to risk and therefore need to consider the part others play and establish clear ethical principles to govern their research (Lomax, 1991b:108-110).

The criteria we suggest against which to judge success in terms of this principle are taken from Lomax (1994c:120). They are that:

❐ the link between reflection and action is established;
❐ the research role is made transparent;
❐ collaborative intent is realised; and
❐ ethical principles governing collaboration are developed, applied and monitored.

Structuring the programme

There are useful strategies that can be employed to make this model of action research work more effectively. The masters programme helps participants to use these strategies and to structure their action research so that they can claim to have achieved some of their objectives and submit a dissertation within a twelve month period.

❑ Within 2–3 months masters students must set up the collaborative support system they need to help them move their work forward. This support system has three elements: a tutorial group in which managers are supported by a tutor; a support set made up of a small group of colleagues from the course; and a critical friend(s) from the work context. Participants are assigned to a tutor group and within that group they must form the smaller support set, but responsibility for recruiting and briefing critical friends is left to them.

❑ By the fourth month masters students must provide an interim report for their tutor and support set in which they justify their concerns, pinpoint educationally worthwhile objectives and outline a feasible plan of action that can be monitored and evaluated.

❑ By the end of nine months masters students will be able to describe and explain their research to a validation group that includes their tutors, support set, critical friend(s) and an independent other, and has been convened specifically for this purpose.

❑ Between the 9th and 12th month masters students should have reflected critically on their work, clarified the criteria against which it should be judged, produced a description and explanation that has been tested out within the support systems available, and presented it as a dissertation for formal assessment within a University.

This structure is based on a system of peer support and peer review. Practitioners' progress at defined points in the programme is supported and evaluated by peers. We believe that collaboration is a key element in success for most students.

Collaborative intent and the critical friend

One strategy for collaborative working is to establish a working relationship with a work colleague who will provide critical but supportive friendship during the period of the research. We call these colleagues critical friends.

We use the term differently to Bayne-Jardine and Holly (1994) who see the critical friend as an outsider process consultant. In our model, the university tutor is most likely to take this role. While we would agree that a critical friend is 'comfortable but challenging, challenging but not threatening' (op.cit:98) we do not see the critical friend as a process consultant. In our model, the critical friend is expected to act as a confidant(e) or mentor and talk through the research at regular intervals, preferably from an insider perspective. Because critical friends are assumed to know the research context well, they can help the researcher deal with the micro politics of work. They may be chosen because their position in their organisation empowers the researcher and adds support to bringing about change. This is seen as a perfectly acceptable situation because we expect researchers to negotiate the focus of their research with senior colleagues so that the work has organisational as well as personal benefit. But the critical friend, who may be a senior colleague, is expected to help the researcher achieve a critical perspective even though this may challenge the normal assumptions underlying the researcher's work. We recognise that such a critical stance is more difficult when the researcher and critical friend share the same values and assumptions. The critical friend is important to the peer review process, because as an insider, with a special knowledge of the research context, s/he is in a position to verify the authenticity of the research. In this role, critical friends attend the validation meeting held at the university, which is part of the formal assessment of the work.

Critical friends' perspectives on the validation meeting

In some earlier, unpublished research, Lomax asked critical friends who had attended validation meetings how they perceived their role in the validation meeting and what contribution they had made. The 26 critical friends who responded to the questions had worked with people registered for the Diploma, In-Service B.Ed. and M.Ed. programmes from 1988-1989. Most respondents described the role of the critical friend at the validation as that of witness, confirming and verifying that the research had taken place in the way in which it was described. They were aware that they, the critical friends, had a direct knowledge of the research context and the work in progress and could give an *objective* account. Some said that they had information to support the validation of their colleagues' research, while others believed themselves to be *evidence* of the claims being made. All but one of the respondents contributed to this description of their role.

Over half the respondents indicated that their role was to give the researcher reassurance and moral support, and a third of the respondents saw their role as helping the researcher present a clearer picture of the research. Although the latter sentiment was mainly about helping the researcher give a good account of the research, for some respondents it seemed to be about defending a position against implied criticism from the tutors who were not aware of the constraints and opportunities facing the researcher in the research context.

A quarter of the respondents viewed their role as having a more evaluative dimension. This was to do with offering an evaluation of 'prior performance', but also having to listen to the evidence at the validation, being ready to agree and disagree, and being willing to contradict the researcher if they thought the claims were not justified. Some saw themselves as giving another viewpoint and speaking for absent colleagues also involved in the research. Respondents stressed that critique needed to be constructive and reference was made to 'critical partnerships'.

In describing how they had verified their colleagues' claims, critical friends used terms like: *proved that, showed that, vouched for and confirmed.* In describing how they had been a witness to the work, many of them spoke of *giving evidence, pointing out, answering questions and giving practical examples.* They claimed to make these comments in the light of their knowledge of the work context, seeing an overview of the context as essential information for being able to judge the success of the project. By painting in the background and raising important questions, critical friends were able to help the researcher clarify aspects of her work for the validation group. This critical support was directed at reminding the researcher about relevant points seen to have been forgotten, helping her to accentuate important points that were felt to be under-emphasised, and clarifying pertinent though peripheral issues. Some of these points were amplified by critical friends into discussions that went beyond the immediate purpose of the meeting. These extended discussions included further explanations of events, other viewpoints, personal opinions, additional information, and placing subjects in a *better* context.

Critical friends described their moral support for the researcher in terms of encouragement, positive feedback and sympathetic support; and three people indicated that they had defended their colleague against invalid criticism. Only one critical friend described how his insider knowledge of the school had enabled him to 'ask more in-depth questions', presumably with the intention of challenging the researcher to provide a better account.

Some critical friends said they played a minor role deliberately so as not to unduly influence their less senior colleagues. Others said they did not know what was expected of them or that there was nothing they could add and so said little.

This analysis formed the basis for the development of new strategies for facilitating students' critical friendships. It is referenced in the paper 'Course Evaluation as Action Research' (Lomax, 1989b:107-108). The results of the research led to more emphasis being placed on advising students about the purpose and briefing of critical friends in the new programmes being developed at that time.

The critical friend as mentor?

Although the small scale enquiry reported above throws some light on the roles that critical friends played during validation meetings, it says little about the relationship of the researcher and critical friend at work. One would expect that at work there is more of a learning and supporting relationship and less of a critical, evaluative relationship. McNiff (1988:84) advises that 'in the initial stages of the enquiry it is essential to attract people who are going to be sympathetic to what you are trying to do ... there will be enough critical reaction later when you come to present your enquiry in the public arena'. Twells (1991:73) says 'A critical friend is someone less critical than your tutor ... an ideal critical friend is someone who is aware of your research, sympathetic to the problems you are encountering, supportive in times of need, but critical when necessary in a constructive helpful manner, and who offers you alternative solutions and values'. Taken out of context, Twells' statement seems more critical of the tutor than was in fact the case, but it does suggest that an essential element in the role of the critical friend during the progress of the research is to do with support. We were struck by the possible affinity of this with the notion of a mentor.

The role of the mentor varies in different contexts and is often negotiable. For some authors, like Wildman *et al.* (1992), it is important to maintain this flexibility. Williams (1993:419), reporting on a survey of 101 teachers from eight different subject areas who were mentoring secondary PGCE students, concluded that 'Current perceptions of strengths and weaknesses reveal a diversity of views which almost certainly reflect not only a wide range of backgrounds and expertise among this group of prospective mentors, but also varied conceptions of the mentor's role and of relative priorities within that role'. Williams' research led her to list six aspects of the mentor's work: organisational, facilitatory, advisory and supportive, observation of teaching, being a role model and assessing (op.cit:415-416).

Reviewing the literature, we found that there are some terms commonly used to describe the mentoring role, such as counsellor, adviser, supervisor, critical friend, staff developer, role model and consultant. These terms mainly refer to the skills required by a mentor. However, knowledge, values and attitudes also need careful consideration.

The mentor-client relationship, like the researcher-critical friend relationship, is a protected relationship in which potential skills are developed. Both are seen to function mainly within a professional context where interpersonal skills are important to their success (Shaw, 1992; Hill *et al.*,1992; Tellez, 1992). Many authors agree that mentoring is about facilitating learning (Clutterbuck, 1987; Watkins and Whalley, 1993; Smith and West-Burnham, 1993) and there is general agreement that mentors are:

❑ influential people who significantly help others reach their major life goals

❑ people whose job involves overseeing the career and development of others outside a normal manager/ subordinate relationship

❑ people at least one step removed, who are concerned with the longer term acquisition and application of skills in a developing career by a form of advising and counselling

❑ people who help others to learn so that their professional roles are enhanced

In some unpublished research, Woodward asked seventeen practising mentors to list the skills that they considered were needed to be an effective mentor. The mentors were working in twenty-six mainstream schools in two authorities in West London. They were experienced teachers who were 'mentoring' newly-qualified teachers in their own schools. The information was collected while they were attending a 'mentor training' top-up course run conjointly by their LEA's and the university. The information was collected midway through a fifteen session course.

The skills of mentoring

The mentors identified a range of skills that Woodward grouped into five categories:

❑ Counselling skills and skills generally associated with a humanistic approach to counselling, such as empathy, reflection, listening and supporting.

❑ Communication skills, including both linguistic competence such as summarising and explaining and interpersonal skills such as listening and negotiating.

❑ Staff development skills, including facilitation (enabling, motivating, encouraging, reflecting, guiding, praising) and coach/manager skills which suggested a more directive approach (leading, evaluating, managing and directing).

❑ Teaching skills, including classroom based skills (classroom management, teaching, subject skills, rapport with pupils) and personal organisational skills (time, resource and stress management).

❑ Personality descriptors, such as pleasant, approachable and discreet.

The literature on mentoring in education suggests a strong consensus about the importance of the first three categories with the exception of the notion of the mentor as coach/manager. This idea is more common in the business literature; indeed Clutterbuck (1987) suggests that mentoring raises the profile of employees, and should be seen as a useful precursor to becoming a manager. Williams (1993) mentioned both classroom teaching skills (op.cit:408-9) and organisational skills (op.cit:415), which could be seen to include some of the skills that are required learning for mentees, and therefore mentors will need some understanding of them (Watkins and Whalley, 1993). They would also be important for the professional credibility of the mentor. The final category identified by Woodward does not refer to skills although it identifies important characteristics for successful mentors.

Evaluating the role of the critical friend

We were interested to see how far these skills were similar to those identified for critical friends. We draw upon questionnaire data in which respondents were asked to identify the work role and gender of their critical friends, explain why they had chosen them and assess the contribution they had made to the research. The questions about critical friends were part of a larger questionnaire intended to enlist participants help in establishing how the M.A. programme had supported their action research in practice (Lomax, 1994b). The questionnaire was returned by 36 out of 44 masters graduates, six months after they had successfully completed the programme. All but 3 of the respondents were school teachers and they included 9 primary school headteachers.

How important were critical friends to the action research enquiries? The majority of respondents said that critical friends were very important to their enquiries, but a substantial minority rated them as only quite important and one person said they were not important. The critical friends chosen were mainly full time work colleagues, mainly women and mainly main grade teachers. A number of critical friends were also from the senior management team (SMT) of the school, again mainly women, although for the SMT the ratio of women to men was 2:1 rather than the 5:1 for critical friends in general. Other critical friends were heads of department, part time teachers, school governors and others from outside the workplace (mainly teachers).

Respondents gave four main reasons for choosing their critical friends. The compatibility of the critical friend was the most frequent reason. This included three dimensions. There were colleagues who shared the researchers' educational values. For example one teacher chose her critical friend because she was positive, child-centred and hard working; another because he was the only member of staff with whom she felt able to discuss educational theory and practice. There were colleagues who could be respected and trusted. For example, one teacher respected her critical friend's professional judgement; another valued her opinion; another felt she would have no worries about revelations or trust; and another that confidentiality would be respected. There were colleagues who could be relied upon to give support. Supportive colleagues included other teachers who taught the same age group, those who would find time to help and one who would support because she 'was naturally enthusiastic about trying to improve practice'.

Another group of reasons for choosing a critical friend was their interest or involvement in the research, or their knowledge about research or the research context. People with an interest in the research were usually people who had a knowledge of the context and shared the researcher's educational values. Often there was a history of discussion about the particular focus of interest because the critical friend had been involved previously with work in that area. More unusually, where a school governor became involved as a critical friend, it was because she had expressed an interest in the work at a governors' meeting and was subsequently approached by the researcher. In another instance, the critical friend was acquired during the course of the research due to common interest in the study. This was similar to the small number of critical friends who were chosen because they were central to the research and presumably shared the research interest. For example one respondent describes how her second critical friend became involved. 'She worked with me at parental meetings and was willing to change her strategies to help me with the action research. She was very enthusiastic about the project. She became more important than my initial critical friend because we were working alongside one another pioneering new strategies. Her cooperation was very important.' Critical friends chosen because they had a knowledge of the context were sometimes close colleagues who understood what the researcher was trying to do or had a similar role, such as where a colleague shared a group of children and naturally took part in discussions of professional matters, or a line manager with whom the teacher regularly discussed relevant issues. At other times they were part of a new context, such as someone who 'played a role in a school where I wanted to develop links' or someone who could help the researcher who was taking up a new job 'to understand my (new) working conditions' and give 'information about the history of the school'. One respondent said that she chose her critical friend because she was 'very aware of the internal politics of the school'. Critical friends were also chosen because of their knowledge of research, particularly action research or because they had done a masters course themselves (and would presumably be sympathetic to the demands involved).

Another reason for choosing a critical friend was that the friend should provide challenging feedback, that she should be a critical friend 'in the true sense' and 'not afraid to tell me the truth about my work'. This notion of challenge was related to characteristics such as the ability to be assertive.

But the need to show sympathetic understanding of the dilemma of the researcher so that criticism was positive rather than negative was also specified. One respondent claimed that her critical friend was 'highly articulate, intelligent and able to give constructive feedback', another that she was 'intelligent, frank and unafraid of confrontation'.

The final reason cited for choosing a critical friend was availability. This included pragmatic reasons such as the critical friend being non class based so that meetings could be held in quality time; and working relations that presented opportunity for frequent discussion such as where the colleague was 'floating' and therefore could support the research by taking part in classroom observation. In some cases the head was chosen for these reasons. Some respondents said that they chose their critical friends because there were no alternatives, such as where they worked in a small staff group.

One might expect that there would be difficulties for headteachers in establishing this relationship in the school because of the head's position of leadership. Of the nine headteachers in the sample, one chose her chair of governors, one a peripatetic teacher who visited the school once a month, and one a headteacher of a local school. All three of these headteachers were new to their posts. The rest (of whom one changed post midway through the research) chose members of staff. Four deputies were chosen (one a senior teacher who became deputy during the course of the research) and four classroom teachers. The head who changed post had a critical friend in both schools. These patterns suggest that established headteachers did not find it a problem to choose a critical friend from their staff. Lack is quite clear about this. '*I was fortunate enough to have a colleague who was to prove an extremely effective 'critical' friend ... One of the criticisms of critical friends is that they are not critical enough, this was not to be a problem in my case*' (Lack, 1992:25). The questionnaire did not include a question to find out what the respondents expected their critical friends to contribute, but the course expectation that critical friends should attend the validation meeting was almost completely met. Girdler provides an interesting insight into the relationship of researcher and critical friend in her account of how her critical friend needed inducting into the role. '*It took time for this level of trust ... that enabled the critical friend to become "critical" in a probing way, asking questions to clarify reasons for actions*' (Girdler, 1992:105). Richards provides an account of how she thought her critical friend *typically* ought to behave: '*getting the drift of what I am trying to say; accepting me for what I am; being interested in me; perceiving what kind of a person I really am, recognising when something is bothering me; and respecting me apart from my skills and status*' (Richards, 1992:61).

Different students offered different rationales for choosing their critical friends and this is compatible with the philosophy of the programme which emphasises the importance of the individual research contexts in determining appropriate strategies. Since this data was gathered changes have been made in the way in which students are introduced to the notion of critical friends and the findings related above form part of their preliminary reading. The philosophy of the programme and the practice of its tutors have also been informed by the development and discussion of six principles of action research (Lomax, 1995a) which are used at the beginning of the programme to organise students' reading and discussion. Two of these principles have clear implications for the way in which students involve critical friends in their research:

❑ that action research is participatory and others are involved as co-researchers rather than informants, so that critical communities of people are formed;
❑ that action research is about sharing ideas, interpretations and conclusions with an 'educated' audience who are able and willing to judge the authenticity and relevance of the work to a particular professional context.

We are not suggesting that these principles are either easily or always achievable, but that all tutors encourage their discussion so that students can interpret and apply them as they see fit within their own situated research. In fact we are moving away from the concept of a critical friend towards one that stresses the importance of a learning relationship (Woodward, 1995). In the final part of this account we would like to give you a glimpse of this sort of relationship. It is taken from the new and very exciting perspective of the self-study of teacher educators (Dadds and Weeks, 1995; Schratz and Schratz-Hadwich, 1995; Lomax and Evans, 1995). We think that the new literature on self-study by teacher educators, where it emphasises the collaborative nature of self-study, could provide considerable insight into the relationship we have defined as critical friendship.

A Learning Relationship or Critical Friendship?

C: My purpose was to develop my understanding of why the learning relationship I have with Z is an effective motivator of learning. I had become dissatisfied with my previous research (reported earlier) where, as an outsider, I investigated the skills required to be an effective mentor. I was also unhappy with most of the texts on mentoring.

An exception is the exciting writing of Buber, whose work suggests to us the possibility of developing a different kind of mentoring relationship. Buber (1975) described two ways in which people can relate to each other. In the I-it relationship we respond to each other as objects and manipulate each other in order to satisfy our own needs. Within this context we are not responding authentically to each other. The other kind of relationship, which is both rarer and more powerful, he calls the I-thou relationship, in which we relate authentically in order to understand each other. He argued that in helping relationships such as the mentor-protégée relationship the more 'mature' of the two should always be extending their authentic 'I'. Buber says that all love and loving relationships have the quality of the I-thou relationship to a greater or lesser degree. Buber underscores that even among those who relate this way there will be many hours of relating to each other as I-its. But the I-thou moments do occur, and these precious times are the primary sources of individual development of each person as human beings. Self-development is a by-product of the I-thou relationship – the stretching to be more because someone believes in your potential.

> C: This interaction was sometimes achieved between Z and myself. When I started working with Z I was not working with any great passion and I was looking for a way to inspire me to research more systematically.

Cathie used a transcript of a taped conversation with Zoe (January 1995) in which they discussed the nature of their learning relationship for further analysis. She was persuaded of the importance of the conversation by Zoe.

> Z: This is a microcosm of our relationship, where it is now .... we can look at the tape, transcribe, analyse, discuss ... '

They agreed with Wildemeersch (1989): 'As conversation is so crucial to everyday life, it is, ipso facto, decisive in relation to education and learning'. They used content analysis (Quinn Patton, 1987) to help analyse the transcript of the tape. They brainstormed the key ideas and discussed them. In addition they engaged in 'micro analysis through collective (or joint) self-reflection' (Schratz, 1993; Schratz, 1994; Schratz and Schratz-Hadwich, 1995). Through these measures they claimed to have developed an understanding of some of the processes involved in researching a learning relationship.

> C: Because we're friends, because we're getting practised at working together, done more things together, we want to develop that into a more formal working together relationship, it's a supportive environment to work with a colleague.

Cathie changed her job, but they continued to talk on the phone: they helped each other maintain the impetus of their enquiries; they supported each other through tricky moments; and they sustained their learning relationship (Treleaven, 1994).

Z: We also like listening to each other's stories ... talk about research narratives.

C: The most important thing with regard to research is the way you encourage me to do it in a way that no one else does so other people tell me to do things and seem to be encouraging but I never feel it's carried through somehow...

Z: We're interested in learning from each other's stories perhaps.

Zoe's presentation of her research as a story (Treleaven, 1994; Evans, 1995b) stimulated Cathie and encouraged her to continue to try to engage with research. It led her to try action research. They both felt it was important that they were peers which made it possible to take risks in a manner that may have been more difficult in a relationship where there was unequal power. In pursuing research, unequal relations such as student-tutor can lead to difficulties for the student (Heinrich, 1991). It is recognised that this could also be the case for unequal relations in the critical friend relationship.'Recent studies of action research projects show a growing awareness of the need for a democratic process that considers each participant's needs, perspectives and skills (Oja and Smulyan, 1989:17).

C: Our solution, within our learning relationship, was to let each other explore ideas that may not have been always seen as directly relevant to the research process.

Z: You had a sense of the importance of your learning the dressage with regard to your Ph.D. and much as people tried to tell you it was irrelevant you still wanted to, not just because it obsessed you but because there is something which is becoming clearer to us ...

It was important for Cathie that Zoe trusted her to understand her own needs to investigate what she called 'a fairly esoteric form of my own learning'. This links to the view that research should concentrate on teachers' lives rather than practices (Goodson and Walker, 1991; Goodson, 1992). Learning conversations were also important. 'Such a conversation is not just chit-chat about disconnected snippets of experience; rather it is a sustained activity creating an increasing awareness of the whole experimental process of learning' (Harri-Augstein and Thomas, 1991:3).

It seems likely that learning relationships are most effective when they are based on strong supportive relationships with established trust between the partners. These facilitate the co-researcher qualities highlighted above.

The account suggests that such relationships allow a great deal of experimentation with ideas and include the possibility for 'critique' that is based on curiosity rather than disapproval.

The consideration of a successful learning relationship provides clues with regard to the practice of critical friendship. It suggests the importance of taking an interest in each other's stories, highlighting the need to trust in and follow where someone leads even if the relevance is not clear. It highlights the importance of developing a sense of shared responsibility. It could support the movement from practice to praxis.

However, we must question whether critical friendship is more effective when it is informal or whether it would benefit from becoming more formalised, with partners contracting to fulfil their part in an agreed process of working together. Where the relationship is not between people of equal status, perhaps contractual arrangements would prevent difficulties caused by different interests.

Conclusion

We have written this chapter in response to the criticism that the model of critical friendship underpinning our support for managers on the M.A. programme is basically flawed, leading to 'collusion' rather than 'critique'. In exploring the data drawn from summative course evaluations, there seems to be no evidence to support this assertion. Respondents to the questionnaires stressed the importance of a putative critical friend's ability to provide challenging or constructive feedback. In-depth questioning was mentioned as part of the critical friend's role. Even with the inequality of power, that is, where the action researcher was managing the critical friend or vice versa, both the researcher and the critical friend claimed they were able to overcome this potential problem so that the 'critical' aspect of the role could be maintained.

The second point to consider is whether collusion is necessarily to be avoided. This is obviously an aspect relating to the critical friend's validation role. There are a variety of professionals involved in the validation process, one of whom is the critical friend. This diverse group of people come together at one of the formative stages of the research and includes other people, such as a university tutor and a support group who maintain close contact over the period of the research, and an independent other who has not been involved at all. Indeed one could argue that the role of the critical friend at the validation meeting is evidential and supportive rather than critical. This does not exclude them from a more critical role in fulfilment of their purpose elsewhere in the research process.

We doubt whether there is a definitive meaning for either 'collusion' or 'critique' within the philosophy of our programme. Students make their own individual claims about their action research and provide evidence that is appropriate to support these. The onus of proof is on the action researcher. The relationship with a critical friend is a formative one and we would suggest that collusion would not impair the educational potential of such a relationship. In fact the evidence from the hermeneutical account of critical friendship presented in the last section suggests that collusion is an important aspect of the relationship, enabling a trust that can be a key motivator in helping the researcher to move forward.

It also seems likely that to dichotomise 'collusion' and 'critique' in the way suggested is too simplistic. Collusion can occur alongside critique, but collusion and critique may both be absent. We are aware that some students do not establish critical friendships at all and some claim to establish them but provide no evidence that they have had any effect on the research. We have no evidence at all that collusion has hindered or invalidated an action research study within the masters programme, but we do have evidence that some of the best action research studies (a judgement supported by external examination) do incorporate critical friendships.

We have highlighted the complexity of the relationships within which the role of the critical friend has meaning and the importance of evaluating these relationships within the situated meanings of the contexts in which they take place. We have seen that the critical friend relationship includes some of the skills and qualities we identified in the mentoring relationship: the need to empower and facilitate learning; the need for someone with an insight into shared context; the need for compatibility and a supportive relationship. There were also some differences. The description of the critical friend included the need for shared experience and the need for a critical partnership, neither of which would usually be included in a description of a mentor.

BIBLIOGRAPHY

Adair, J. (1983) *Effective Leadership*, London: Pan.

Adair, J. (1984) *The Skills of Leadership*, Aldershot: Gower.

Adelman, C. (1989) 'The practical ethic takes priority over methodology' in (ed.) W. Carr *Quality in Teaching*, London: Falmer Press, 173-182.

Alexander, R. (1992) *Policy and Practice in Primary Education*, London: Routledge.

Altrichter, H. (1992) 'The concept of quality in action research: giving practitioners a voice in educational research' in (ed.) M.Schratz *Qualitative Voices in Educational Research*, London: Falmer Press, 40-50.

Anyon, J. (1983) 'Intersections of Gender and Class and accommodation and resistance by working class and affluent females to contradictory sex-role ideologies' in (ed.) S. Walker and L. Barton, *Gender Class and Education*, Lewes: Falmer Press. 19-37.

Aspin, D., Chapman, J. and Wilkinson, V. (1994) *Quality Schooling*, London: Cassell.

Baggaley, S. (1992) 'Hospital and Home Tuition', School Science Review 74 (266), 140-141.

Barnes, D. (1992) 'The significance of teachers' frames for teaching' in (eds) T. Russell and H. Munby, *Teachers and Teaching: From Classroom to Reflection*, New York: Falmer Press.

Bayne-Jardine, C. and Holly, P. (1994) *Developing Quality Schools* London: The Falmer Press.

Belasco, J.A. and Alluto, J.A. (1972) 'Decisional participation and teacher satisfaction' in *Educational Administration Quarterly* 8 (1) 36-37.

Belbin, M. (1985) *Management Teams*, London: Heinemann.

Belenky, M., Clinchy, B., Goldberger, N. and Tarule, J. (1986) *Women's Ways of Knowing*, New York: Basic Books.

Bell, G. (1987) 'Using action research enquiry' in *British Journal of In-Service Education* 14 (1)

Bone, D. (1993) *How can I develop a collegiate management style in the school and encourage the senior management team to involve staff fully?* M.Ed. Dissertation, Kingston University.

BP Chemicals (1992), *'Total Quality Management'*.

Brunt, M.P. (1989) 'Marketing Schools' in (ed.) I.Craig, *Primary School Management in Action*, London: Longman, 224-241.

Buber, M. (1975) *I and Thou* Edinburgh: Clark.

Bush, T. (1986) *Theories of Educational Management*, London: Harper and Row.

Carr, W. and Kemmis, S. (1986) *Becoming Critical: Education, Knowledge and Action Research* Lewes: Falmer Press.

Carter, K. (1990) 'Teachers' knowledge and learning to teach' in (ed.) W.R. Houston, *Handbook of Research on Teacher Education*, New York: Macmillan, 291-310.

Carter, K. (1993) 'The place of story in the study of teaching and teacher education' *Educational Researcher*, 22 (1) 5-12,18.

Carter, K. and Doyle, W. (1987) 'Teachers' knowledge structures and comprehension processes' in (ed.) J. Calderhead, *Exploring Teachers' Thinking*, London: Cassell, 147-160.

Carter, K. and Gonzales, L. (1990) 'Teachers' knowledge of classrooms and classroom events', a paper presented at the American Educational Research Association Annual Meeting, Boston.

Chafe, W. (1990) 'Some things that narratives tell us about the mind' in (eds) B.K. Briteen and A.D. Pellegrini *Narrative Thought and Narrative Language*, New Jersey: Lawrence Erlbaum Associates, 79-98.

Clarricoates, K. (1980) 'The Importance of being Ernest ... Emma ... Tom ... Jane ... ' in (ed.) R. Deem, *Schooling for Women's Work*, London: Routledge, 26-42.

Clutterbuck, D. (1987) 'Everyone Needs a Mentor', Institute of Personnel Managers.

Cochran-Smith, M. and Lytle, S. (1990) 'Research on teaching and teacher research: the issues that divide' in *Educational Researcher*, 19 (2) 2-11.

Cole, A. and Knowles, J.G. (1994) 'Personal histories, professional practices: methods and examples of self study', a paper presented at the American Educational Research Association Annual Meeting, New Orleans.

Collard, R. (1989) *Total Quality: Success Through People*, London: Institute of Personnel Managers.

Connelly, M. and Clandinin, J. (1990) 'Stories of experience and narrative enquiry' in *Educational Researcher*, 19 (5) 2-14.

Convery, A. (1993) 'Developing fictional writing as a means of stimulating teacher reflection' in *Educational Action Research*, 1 (1) 135-151.

Crawford, J., Kippax, S., Onyx, J., Gault, U. and Benton, P. (1992) *Emotion and Gender*, London: Sage.

CSCS (1986) *Broadsheet 17 : Schools in the Market-Place*, Northampton Centre for the Study of Comprehensive Schools.

D'Arcy, P. (1994) 'Knocking down the Aunt Sallys: a response to Martyn Hammersley' in *Educational Action Research* 2 (2) 291-293.

Dadds, M. and Weeks, P. (1995) 'Conversation Five: the feeling of thinking in professional self study' in (ed.) T. Ghaye, *Creating Cultures for Improvement: Dialogues, Decisions and Dilemmas*, Bournemouth: Hyde Publications.

Davies, B., Ellison, L., Osborne, A. and West-Burnham, J. (1990) *Education Management for the 1990s*, Harlow: Longman.

Deem, R. (1980) *Schooling for Women's Work*, London: Routledge.

Delandshere, G. and Petrosky, A. (1994) 'Capturing teachers' knowledge: performance assessment' in *Educational Researcher*, 23 (5) ll-18.

Department For Education (1994) 'Pupils with problems:the education of sick children', Circular 12/94, HMSO: London.

Department For Education (1994) 'Code of Practice on the Identification and Assessment of Special Educational Needs', HMSO: London.

Department For Education and National Health Service (1994) Circular 12/94, HMSO: London.

Department For Education (1995) *Science in the National Curriculum*, HMSO: London.

Department of Education and Science (1991)*Education and Training for the Twenty-First Century*, London: HMSO.

Dewey, J. (1916) *Essays in Experimental Logic*, New York: Dover.

Dewsbury, M. and Jones, A. (1984) 'Science teaching at the bedside' in *Special Education*, 11 (1), 35-37.

Doherty, G. (1994) *Developing Quality Systems in Education*, London: Routledge.

Education Act (1993) Cap 35, HMSO: London.

Eisner, E.W. (1993) 'Forms of Understanding and the Future of Educational Research' in *Educational Researcher*, 22 (7) 5-11.

Evans, M. (1993) *An action research enquiry into my role as a deputy headteacher in a comprehensive school*, Transfer report from M.Phil to Ph.D., Kingston University.

Evans, M. (1995a) 'Let the action begin' in *Forum* 37 (3) 84-86.

Evans, M. (1995b) *An action research enquiry into reflection in action as part of my role as a deputy headteacher*, Ph.D. Thesis, Kingston: Kingston University.

Fenstermacher, G.G. (1992) 'Where are we going? Who will lead us there?' Address to the Annual Meeting of the American Association of Colleges of Teacher Education.

FEU (1991) *Quality Matters: Business and Industry Quality Models and Further Education*, Kettering: Premier Print Limited.

Fiddler, B. and Bowles, G. (1991) *Effective Local Management of Schools Workbook: Planning your school's strategy*, Harlow: Longman.

Fletcher, M. (1991) 'In the market for understanding', *Times Educational Supplement*, 13th September 1991.

Forward, D. (1989) 'Action Research', in (ed.) P. Lomax, *The Management of Change*, Clevedon: Multi-Lingual Matters, 29-39.

Foucault, M. (1977) 'Intellect and power' in (ed.) D.F. Bouchard, *Michel Foucault, Language, Counter-Memory, Practice*, Oxford: Basil Blackwell.

Foucault, M. (1980) *Power/Knowledge: Selected Interviews and other writings 1972-1977*, translated and edited by C. Gordon, New York: Pantheon.

Fox, L., Brody, I. and Tobin, D. (1977) *Women and Mathematical Mystique*, John Hopkins University Press.

Friends Workshop Group (1985) *Ways and Means: An approach to problem solving* Kingston Friends Workshop Group, 78 Eden Street, Kingston-upon-Thames KT1 2BJ.

Fullan, M. (1992) *Successful School Improvement*, Buckingham: Open University Press.

Gadamer, H. (1975) *Truth and Method*, London: Sheed and Ward.

Genovese, E. (1983) 'Intersections of Gender and Class' in (ed.) L. Barton and S. Walker, *Gender Class and Education*, Lewes: Falmer Press, 21-23.

Ghaye, T. and Wakefield, P. (1993) *The Role of Self in Action Research*, Bournemouth: Hyde Publications.

Girdler, C. (1992) *How can I develop a structure for teaching and ancillary staff to work within that will enable the learning of statemented children to be enhanced?* Unpublished M.A. Dissertation, Kingston University.

Glatter, R., Preedy, M., Riches, C. and Masterton, M. (1988) *Understanding School Management*, Milton Keynes: OU Press.

Goodson, I. (1992) *Studying Teachers' Lives*, London: Routledge.

Goodson, I. and Walker, R. (1991) *Biography, Identity and Schooling:Episodes in Educational Research*, Basingstoke: Falmer.

Gray, L. (1989) 'Marketing Education Services' in (ed.) R. Glatter, *Educational Institutions and their Environments: Managing the Boundaries*, Buckingham: Open University Press: 48-62.

Greenwood, M. and Gaunt, J. (1994) *Total Quality Management for Schools*, London: Cassell.

Griffiths, M. (1990) 'Action Research: grassroots practice or management tool?' in (ed.) P. Lomax, *Managing Staff Development in Schools*, Clevedon: Multi-Lingual Matters.

Gurney, M. (1989) 'Implementor or Innovator? A teacher's challenge to the restrictive paradigm of traditional research' in (ed.) P. Lomax, *The Management of Change*, Clevedon: Multi-Lingual Matters, 13-28.

Habermas, J. (1976) *Communication and the Evolution of Society*, London: Routledge.

Hammersley, M. (1993) 'On the teacher as researcher' in (ed.) M. Hammersley, *Educational Research: Current Issues*, London: Paul Chapman Publishing, 211-231.

Handy, C. (1989) *The Age of Unreason*, London: Arrow Books.

Hannon, D. (1995) 'Science Boxes For Children Being Taught At Home Or In Hospital', Kingston University: Kingston Upon Thames.

Hardie, B. (1991) *Marketing the Primary School*, United Kingdom: Northcote House Publishers Ltd.

Hargreaves, A. (1995) 'Beyond collaboration: critical teacher development in the post modern age' in (ed.) J. Smyth, *Critical Discourse on Teacher Development*, London: Cassell.

Harri-Augustein, S. and Thomas, L. (1991) *Learning Conversations*, London: Routledge.

Harrison, M. and Gill, S. (1992) *Primary School Management*, London: Heinemann Educational.

Haug, F. *et al.* (1987) *Female Sexualisation: a Collective Work on Memory*, London: Verso.

Heinrich, K.T. (1991) 'Loving partnerships: dealing with sexual attraction and power in doctoral advisement relationships' in *Journal of Higher Education*, 6 (5) 514-538.

Hellawell, D. (1992) 'Spreading the load' in *School Management Today*, Volume 2 (2) 20-24.

Hill, A., Jenning, M. and Madgewick, B. (1992) 'Initiating a mentorship training programme' in (ed.) M. Wilkin, *Mentoring in Schools*, London: Kogan Page.

Hodgkinson, C. (1983) *The Philosophy of Leadership*, Oxford: Basil Blackwell.

Holley, E. (1995) 'What is Good Quality Educational Research?' in *Action Researcher* 4.

Hopkins, D. (1987) *A Teacher's Guide to Classroom Research*, Buckingham: OU Press.

Kelly, R. (1991) 'In praise of followers' in *Harvard Business Review, Managers as Leaders*, Boston: Harvard Business School Press, 84-94.

Kemmis, S. and Henry, C. (1984) *A Point by Point Guide to Action Research*, Australia: Deakin University Press.

Kessler, S. and McKenna, W. (1982) 'Developmental aspects of gender' in (ed.) E. Whitelegg, *The Changing Experience of Women*, Oxford: Blackwell, Kingston

Kirby, S. (1989) 'Hospital teaching developments during 1989' in *Links* 15, 22-23.

Kotter, J.P. (1990) 'Leadership' in *The Independent*, 10th June 1990.

Kotter, J.P. (1991) 'What leaders really do' in *Harvard Business Review, Managers as Leaders*, Boston: Harvard Business School Press, 3-12.

Lack, M. (1992) 'How can I improve the behaviour of children in the playground?' Unpublished M.A. Dissertation, Kingston University.

Lawrence, D. (1988) Lawseq Self-esteem questionnaire, p15, *Enhancing Self-Esteem in the Classroom*, London: Paul Chapman.

Lewis, R. and Smith, D.H. (1994) *Total Quality in Higher Education*, Florida: St Lucie Press.

Lloyd, D. and Archer, I. (eds) (1976) *Exploring Sex Differences*, London: Academic Press.

Loftus, J. (1991) 'Bringing about a more effective working relationship between teaching and ancillary staff in an infant school' in (ed.) P. Lomax, *Managing Better Schools and Colleges: An Action Research Way*, Clevedon: Multi-Lingual Matters, 44-53.

Lomax, P. (1986a) 'Action researchers' action research: a symposium' in *Journal of In-Service Education* 13 (1) 42-49.

Lomax, P. (1986b) 'Teachers' in-service career patterns' in *Research Papers in Education* 1 [2] 123-136.

Lomax, P. (1987) 'The political implications of defining relevant INSET' in *European Journal of Teacher Education* 10 [2] 221-229.

Lomax, P. (1989a) *The Management of Change*, Clevedon: Multi Lingual Matters, 183 pages.

Lomax, P. (1989b) 'An action research approach to course evaluation' in (ed.) P. Lomax, *The Management of Change*, Clevedon: Multi Lingual Matters, 99-113.

Lomax, P. (1990a) *Managing Staff Development in Schools*, Clevedon: Multi Lingual Matters.

Lomax, P. (1990b) 'An action research approach to developing staff in schools' in (ed.) P. Lomax, *Managing Staff Development in Schools*, Clevedon: Multi-Lingual Matters, 2-7.

Lomax, P. (1990c) 'The role of the teacher researcher' in (ed.) P. Lomax, *Managing Staff Development in Schools*, Clevedon: Multi Lingual Matters, 1-6.

Lomax, P. (1990d) 'Publish or be damned: a conversation' in *Research Intelligence* 34, 1990.

Lomax, P. (1991a) *Managing Better Schools and Colleges*, Clevedon: Multi Lingual Matters, 119 pages

Lomax, P. (1991b) 'Peer review and action research' in (ed.) P. Lomax, *Managing Better Schools and Colleges: An Action Research Way*, Clevedon: Multi-Lingual Matters, 102-113.

Lomax, P. (1992) 'Using action research to improve curriculum and instruction: two case studies from British schools' in *Educational Research Journal*, a publication of the Hong Kong Educational Research Association, Vol 7, August 1992.

Lomax, P. (1993) 'Managing change and the empowerment of schools' in (ed.) H. Busher and M. Smith, *Managing Institutional Development*, Sheffield: Hallam University, 105-117.

Lomax, P. (1994a) 'Management training for schools and colleges' in (eds) P. Lomax and J. Darley, *Management Research in the Public Sector*, Bournemouth: Hyde Publications, 1-28.

Lomax, P. (1994b) 'Action research for managing change' in (eds) N. Bennett, R. Glatter and R. Levacic, *Improving Educational Management through Research and Consultancy*, London: Paul Chapman, 156-167.

Lomax, P. (1994c) 'Standards, criteria and the problematic of action research' in *Educational Action Research*, 2 (1) 113-125.

Lomax, P. (1994d) *The Narrative of an Educational Journey or Crossing the Tracks*, inaugural address, Kingston University, 1-24.

Lomax, P. (1995a) 'Action research for professional practice' in *British Journal of In-Service Education* 21(1)1-9.

Lomax, P. (1995b) 'In search of a model of continuing professional development for primary school teachers', invited paper, Annual Conference of the Hong Kong Educational Research Association, Hong Kong, 1995.

Lomax, P. and Cowan, J. (1989) 'Reflecting on the action: questions of assessment and accreditation' in (ed.) P. Lomax, *The Management of Change*, Clevedon: Multi Lingual Matters , 114-129.

Lomax, P. and Darley, J. (1994) *Management Research in the Public Sector*, Bournemouth: Hyde Publications.

Lomax, P. and Darley, J. (1995) 'Inter-school links, liaisons and networking: collaboration or competition?' in *Educational Management and Administration*, Volume 23 (3).

Lomax, P. and Evans, M. (1995) 'Working in partnership to implement teacher research', a paper presented at the American Educational Research Association Annual Meeting, San Francisco 1995.

Lomax, P. and Evans, M. (1996) 'Working in partnership to enhance self-study within teacher education', a paper presented at the American Educational Research Association, New York.

Lomax, P. and Jones, C. (1993a) *Developing the Primary School to Implement National Curriculum Key Stage 1 Assessment: action research case studies*, Bournemouth: Hyde Publications.

Lomax, P. and Jones, C. (1993b) 'Seven years on in an assessment community' in (eds) P. Lomax and C. Jones, *Developing the Primary School to Implement National Curriculum Key Stage 1 Assessment: action research case studies*, Bournemouth: Hyde Publications, 1-12.

Lomax, P. and McLeman, P. (1984) 'The uses and abuses of nominal group technique in course evaluation' in *Studies in Higher Education* 9 (2) 183-190.

Lomax, P. and Parker, Z. (1995) 'Accounting for ourselves: the problematic of representing action research' in *Cambridge Journal of Education*, Volume 25 (3) 301-314.

MacLure, M. (1993) 'Arguing for your self: identity as an organising principle in teachers' jobs and lives' in *British Journal of Educational Research*, 19 (4).

MacNeile-Dixoñ, R. (1939) *The Human Situation*, London: Penguin.

Mann, S. and Pedler, M. (1992) 'Editorial' in *Journal of Management Education and Development* 23 (3) 181-183.

Marsh, D.T. (1989) *An Introduction to Leadership and its Functions in Further and Higher Education*, Bristol: The Staff College.

McNiff, J. (1988) *Action Research: Principles and Practices*, London and New York: Routledge.

McNiff, J. (1993) *Teaching as Learning: an action research approach*, London and New York: Routledge.

McNiff, J., Whitehead, J. and Laidlaw, M. (1992) *Creating a Good Social Order through Action Research*, Bournemouth: Hyde Publications.

McRobbie, A. (1978) 'Settling accounts with sub-cultures: a feminist critique' in *Screen Education* 34:37-8

Moss, P. (1994) 'Can there be validity without reliability?' in *Educational Researcher*, 23(2) 6-12.

Murgatroyd, S. and Morgan, C. (1993) *Total Quality Management in Schools*, Buckingham: Open University Press.

Nicholas, M. (1991) 'Gender dynamics and support teaching: an action research experiment in a multi-ethnic middle school' in (ed.) P. Lomax, *Managing Better Schools and Colleges: An Action Research Way*, Clevedon: Multi-Lingual Matters, 33-43.

Nicholson, J. (1992) *How Do You Manage?* London: BBC Books.

Oakley, A. (1990) *Housewife*, Harmondsworth: Penguin.

Oja, S. and Smulyan, L. (1989) *Collaborative Action Research: A Developmental Approach*, Basingstoke: Falmer.

Parrott, A. (1995) Book review, H.Skolimowski, *The Participatory Mind*, Penguin, in *Collaborative Inquiry*, 16, Centre for Action Research in Professional Practice, University of Bath.

Parsons, C. (1994) *Quality Improvement in Education*, David Fulton Publishers.

Pascale, R. (1990) *Managing on the Edge*, London: Viking.

Peters, T.J. (1988) *Thriving on Chaos: Handbook for a Management Revolution*, London: Guild Publishing.

Peters, T.J. and Waterman, R.H. (1982) *In Search of Excellence*, New York: Harper and Row.

Pimenoff, S. (1995) 'Time to act' in *The Guardian*, April 11th 1995, p14.

Prospect Centre (1991) *Growing an Innovative Workforce*, London: The Prospect Centre.

Quinn Patton, M. (1987) *How To Use Qualitative Methods in Evaluation*, London: Sage Publications.

Randall, G. (1987) 'Gender differences in pupil-teacher interaction in workshops and laboratories' in (eds) G. Weiner and M. Arnot, *Gender Under Scrutiny*, Bucks: Open University Press, 163-172.

Reason, R. and Rowan, J. (1981) *Human Enquiry*, London: Wiley.

Richardson, V. (1994) 'Conducting research on practice' in *Educational Researcher*, 23(5) 5-10.

Richards, T. (1992) 'The implementation of the recommendations outlined in a whole school inspection report', unpublished M.A. Dissertation, Kingston University.

Riley, K. and Nuttall, D. (1994) *Measuring Quality*, London: The Falmer Press.

Roberts, R. (1991) 'A modestly positive way forward through action research' in *British Journal of In-service Education* 17 (1)45.

Russell, T. and Munby, H. (1992) *Teachers and Teaching: from classroom to reflection*, New York: Falmer Press.

Russell, U. (1990) *Promoting a Positive Image*, London: Industrial Society.

Ryan, H. (1992) 'Conflicting values: managing the tensions' in *Educational Management and Administration* 20 (4) 259-264.

Sayers, J. (1987) 'Psychology and gender divisions' in (eds) G. Weiner and M. Arnot, *Gender Under Scrutiny*, Bucks: Open University Press, 163-172.

Schön, D.A. (1983) *The Reflective Practitioner: How Professionals Think in Action*, New York: Basic Books.

Schratz, M. (1993a) *Qualitative Voices in Educational Research*, London: Falmer Press.

Schratz, M. (1993b) 'Researching while teaching: promoting reflective professionality in higher education' in *Educational Action Research* 1 [1].

Schratz, M. (1994) 'Collaborative, self-critical and reciprocal inquiry through memory-work': Draft paper presented at the third World Congress on *Action Learning, Action Research and Process Management*, University of Bath, July 1994.

Schratz, M. and Schratz-Hadwich, B. (1995) 'Collective memory work: the self as a re/source for re/search' in (eds) M. Schratz and R.Walker, *Research as Social Change*, London: Routledge.

Shave, S. (1978) 'Ten ways to counter sexism in a Junior School' in *Spare Rib* 75 p.42.

Shaw, R. (1992) *Teacher Training in Secondary Schools*, London: Kogan Page.

Simon, B. and Willcocks, J. (eds) (1981) *Research and Practice in the Primary Classroom*, London: Routledge.

Skolimowski, H. (1992) *Living Philosophy*, London: Penguin.

Skolimowski,H. (1994) *The Participatory Mind*, London: Penguin.

Smith, M. and West-Burnham, J. (1993) *Mentoring in the Effective School*, London: Longman.

Southworth, G. (1988) 'Primary Headship and Collegiality' in (eds) R. Glatter, M. Preedy, M.C. Riches, and M. Masterton, *Understanding School Management*,Milton Keynes: Open University, pp.45-56.

Spender, D. (1982) *Invisible Women: The Schooling Scandal*, London: The Women's Press.

Stanworth, M. (1987) 'Girls on the margins: a study of gender divisions in the classroom' in (eds) G. Weiner and M. Arnot, *Gender Under Scrutiny*, Bucks: Open University Press, 26-36.

Stenhouse, L. (1975) *An Introduction to Curriculum Research and Development*, London: Heinemann.

Stenhouse, L. (1983) *Authority, Education and Emancipation*, London: Heinemann.

Stott, K. and Parr, H. (1991) *Marketing your School*, London: Hodder and Stoughton.

Tannenbaum, R. and Schmidt, W. (1991) 'How to choose a leadership pattern' in *Harvard Business Review, Managers as Leaders,* Boston: Harvard Business School Press, 25-34.

Tasker, M. and Packham, D. (1993) 'Industry and higher education: a question of values' in *Studies in Higher Education,* 18 (2) 127-136.

Tellez, K. (1992) 'Mentors by choice not design: help seeking by beginning teachers' in *Journal of Teacher Education* 43 (3) 214-221.

Torbert, W. (1981) 'Why educational research has been so uneducational: the case for a new model of social science based on collaborative enquiry' in (eds) P. Reason and J. Rowan, *Human Enquiry,* London: Wiley.

Treleaven, L. (1994) 'Making a Space: a Collaborative Inquiry with Women as Staff Development' in (ed.) P. Reason, *Participation in Human Inquiry,* London: Sage, 138-162.

Trethowan, D. (1985) *The Leadership of Schools,* London: Education for Industrial Society.

Tripp, D. (1993) *Critical Incidents in Teaching,* London: Routledge.

TTA (Teacher Training Agency) (1995) 'Teacher Training Agency initial advice to the Secretary of State on the continuing professional development of teachers', TTA paragraph 11.

Twells, B. (1991) 'Developing my role as a science co-ordinator in a primary school' in (ed.) P. Lomax, *Managing Better Schools and Colleges: An Action Research Way,* Clevedon: Multi-Lingual Matters, 70-81.

van Manen, M. (1995) 'On the Epistemology of Reflective Practice' in *Teachers and Teaching: Theory and Practice* 1 (1)33-50.

Vulliamy, G. and Webb, R. (1991) 'Teacher research and educational change: an empirical study' in *British Educational Research Journal* 17 (3) 219-236.

Walker, R. (1981) 'On the uses of fiction in educational research' in D. Smetherham (ed.) *Practising Education,* Driffield: Nafferton, 157-163.

Walker, R. (1993) 'Finding a silent voice for the researcher: using photographs in evaluation and research' in (ed.) M. Schratz, *Qualitative Voices in Educational Research,* Falmer Press: London, 72-92.

Wallace, C. (1987) 'From girls and boys to women and men: the social reproduction of gender' in (ed.) G. Weiner and M. Arnot , *Gender and the Politics of Schooling,* London: Hutchinson, 237-250.

Watkins, C. and Whalley, C. (1993) *Mentoring: Resources for School Based Learning,* London: Longman.

Webb, R. (1991) 'Practitioner research and the national curriculum: a personal view' in (ed.) C. O'Hanlon, *Participatory Enquiry in Action,* CARN Bulletin No. 10A, University of East Anglia, 17-37.

Weiner, G. and Arnot, M. (1987) 'Teachers and Gender Politics' in (eds) in G.Weiner and M. Arnot, *Gender and the Politics of Schooling,* Bucks: Open University Press, 79-87.

West-Burnham, J. (1990) 'Human resource management in schools' in (eds) B. Davies, L. Ellison, A. Osborne and J. West-Burnham, *Education Management for the 1990s,* London:Longman, 64-92.

West-Burnham, J. (1992) *Managing Quality in Schools*, London: Longman.

West-Burnham, J. and Davies, B. (1994) 'Quality management as a response to educational change', a paper presented at the American Educational Research Association annual meeting, New Orleans.

West, M. and Ainscow, M. (1991) *Managing School Development: a Practical Guide*, London: David Fulton.

West, S. (1993) *Educational Values for School Leadership*, London: Kogan Page.

Wexler, P. (1995) 'After postmodernism: a new age social theory in Education', in (eds) R. Smith and P. Wexler, *After Postmodernism*, London: Falmer.

Whitehead, J. (1982) 'Assessing and evaluating an individual's educational development' in *Assessment and Evaluation in Higher Education*, 7 (1) 22-27.

Whitehead, J. (1985) 'An analysis of an individual's educational development: the basis for personally orientated action research' in (ed.) M. Shipman, *Educational Research: Principles and Practices*, Basingstoke: Falmer Press.

Whitehead, J. (1989) 'Creating a living educational theory from questions of the kind, How do I improve my practice?' in *Cambridge Journal of Education* 19 (1) 41-52.

Whitehead, J. (1993) *The Growth of Educational Knowledge: creating your own living educational theories*, Bournemouth: Hyde Publications.

Whitehead, J. and Foster, D. (1984) 'Action research and professional educational development', *CARN Bulletin No. 6*, University of East Anglia, 41-44.

Whitehead, J. and Lomax, P. (1987) 'The politics of educational knowledge' in *British Educational Research Journal* 13 (3) 175-190.

Wildemeersch, D. (1989) '*The Principal Meaning of Dialogue for the Construction and Transformation of Reality*' in (ed.) S.W. Weil and J. McGill, *Making Sense of Experiential Learning: Diversity in Theory*, Buckingham: Open University Press, 60-69.

Wildman, P. (1995) 'Research by looking backwards: reflective praxis as an action research model' in *ARCS Newsletter* 13 (1) 20-38.

Wildman, T., Magliaro, S., Niles, R. and Niles, J. (1992) 'Teacher mentoring: an analysis of roles, activities and conditions' in *Journal of Teacher Education*, 43 (3) 205-213.

Wiles, P. (1988) 'Teaching children in hospital' in *British Journal of Special Education*, 15 (4)158-162.

Williams, A. (1993) 'Teacher perceptions of their needs as mentors in the context of developing school-based initial teacher education' in *British Educational Research Journal*, 19 (4) 407-420.

Wilson, K. (1993) 'Education of hospitalised children' in *Paediatric Nursing*, 5 (4) 23-25.

Winter, R. (1987) 'Collaboration' in '*The Dialectics of Practice and Reflection in Action Research*', CARN Bulletin 8, 109-116.

Winter, R. (1989) *Learning from Experience*, London: The Falmer Press.

Winter, R. (1991) 'Interviews, interviewees and the exercise of power' in *British Educational Research Journal*, 17 (3) 251-262.

Woodward, C. (1995) 'A learning relationship: one voice', a paper presented at the European Conference on Educational Research, University of Bath.

Zuber-Skerritt, O. (1991) 'Management Development through Action Learning and Action Research' in *ETTI* 27 (4) 437-447.